THE DIVERGENT COMPANION

Dark Fusions: Where Monsters Lurk! *(editor)*

The Mortal Instruments Companion: City of Bones, Shadowhunters, and the Sight: The Unauthorized Guide

Eldritch Evolutions

The Hunger Games Companion

Blood and Ice

The Twilight Companion: The Unauthorized Guide to the Series

The Fan's Guide to Artemis Fowl

The Fan's Guide to The Spiderwick Chronicles: Unauthorized Fun with Fairies, Ogres, Brownies, Boggarts, and More!

Exploring Philip Pullman's His Dark Materials: An Unauthorized Adventure Through The Golden Compass, The Subtle Knife, and The Amber Spyglass

The Ultimate Unauthorized Eragon Guide: The Hidden Facts Behind the World of Alagaesia

The Truth Behind a Series of Unfortunate Events: Eyeballs, Leeches, Hypnotism, and Orphans—Exploring Lemony Snicket's World

Dragonball Z: An Unauthorized Guide

Nightfall

The Termination Node *(with Robert Weinberg)*

The Computers of Star Trek *(with Robert Weinberg)*

Technolife 2020 (fiction and fact)

Chuck Farris and the Tower of Darkness

Chuck Farris and the Cosmic Storm

Chuck Farris and the Labyrinth of Doom

The Science of Superheroes *(with Robert Weinberg)*

The Science of Supervillains *(with Robert Weinberg)*

The Science of James Bond *(with Robert Weinberg)*

The Science of Anime *(with Robert Weinberg)*

The Science of Stephen King *(with Robert Weinberg)*

Did It Have to Be Snakes? From Science to the Supernatural, the Many Mysteries of Indiana Jones *(with Robert Weinberg)*

The
DIVERGENT
COMPANION

THE UNAUTHORIZED GUIDE
TO THE SERIES

Lois H. Gresh

ST. MARTIN'S GRIFFIN ✒ NEW YORK

www.stmartins.com

Library of Congress Cataloging-in-Publication Data

Gresh, Lois H.
  The Divergent companion : the unauthorized guide to the series / Lois H. Gresh.—First edition.
       p. cm.
   ISBN 978-1-250-04510-2 (trade paperback)
   ISBN 978-1-4668-4351-6 (e-book)
   1. Roth, Veronica. Divergent.   2. Roth Veronica—Handbooks, manuals, etc.   I. Title.
   PS3618.O8633Z68 2014
   813'.6—dc23

                                        2013048567

St. Martin's Griffin books may be purchased for educational, business, or promotional use. For information on bulk purchases, please contact Macmillan Corporate and Premium Sales Department at 1-800-221-7945, extension 5442, or write specialmarkets@macmillan.com.

FIRST EDITION: February 2014

10 9 8 7 6 5 4 3 2 1

CONTENTS

WHAT'S IN
THIS BOOK?

Welcome to *The Divergent Companion*! In this book, you'll learn all about the backbones of the *Divergent* world created by Veronica Roth. By now, you may have seen the movie, due in theaters from Summit Entertainment–Lions Gate in March 2014. Or you may be anticipating the *Divergent* film while reading the trilogy of novels for the third or fourth time.

Because this is a *companion* to the world of *Divergent*, I assume that you've already read the three books, *Divergent, Insurgent,* and *Allegiant.* Hence, I don't tell you what you already know: the chronology of events, what characters explicitly say and do, and so forth. Instead, I fill in all the gaps and answer your questions about how this world might work and why things might happen as they do.

You'll learn the answers to burning questions, such as:

- Do the factions actually make sense? Do we have factions in the real world, and if so, what are they?
- Are we all more Divergent than we think?
- How might the serums and transmitters work? Are they at all realistic?
- How far away are we in the real world to the genetic manipulations in *Allegiant*?
- Is it possible to change an entire population and alter the way everybody thinks by toying with genes?
- Are mirror neurons real, and do they make people think in a more divergent fashion?
- What does creativity have to do with the Divergent?
- How is Tris's brain really wired?
- Is it true, as Tris worries, that the size of our brain sections determines who we are and what we do, that our brain anatomy defines our entire personalities?
- What is the Milgram experiment, and how does it tie in to the events of the Divergent trilogy?
- How do the serums and neurotransmitters *really* work? Is all this possible?
- How do the simulations *really* work? Are *they* possible?
- How does a simulation induce fear in somebody?
- Can two people be inside the same simulation at the same time?

and much more.

The *Divergent* film features Shailene Woodley in the role of Tris Prior and twenty-eight-year-old Theo James as Tobias/Four. At five feet eight inches, Shailene Woodley is taller than I imagined the tiny Tris, but remarkably, her face reminds me of how I envisioned Tris while reading the trilogy. She's twenty-one years old and already has an impressive list of acting credentials. Academy Award–winner Kate Winslet, famous for her roles in movies such as *Titanic* with Leonardo DiCaprio, plays Jeanine Matthews, the leader of the Erudite faction. With a cold sharpness, she brings an edge to the character.

The author of the *Divergent* series, Veronica Roth, grew up in Barrington, Illinois, and now lives in Chicago with her husband, Nelson Fitch. She was born in 1988 and achieved phenomenal literary success at a very young age. Her work has won accolades such as *New York Times* Bestseller, *USA Today* Bestseller, *Publishers Weekly* Best Book, and *School Library Journal* Best Book. As of this writing, the first two novels in the series have sold more than three million copies.[1]

Now that the *Divergent* trilogy has come to a close, fans await news about Veronica Roth's next project while eagerly reading her e-stories about Tobias/Four. In addition, you can settle back, flip to the next page, and start discovering all the gritty details behind the world of *Divergent*!

VERSIONS OF THE NOVELS REFERENCED IN THIS BOOK

Divergent. New York: HarperCollins, first paperback edition, 2011.

Insurgent. New York: HarperCollins, first hardcover edition, 2012.

Allegiant. New York: HarperCollins, first hardcover edition, 2013.

FACTIONS AND
FREE WILL

We're all born into factions of some kind. Our grandparents or parents may be immigrants from another country, they may be of a particular ethnicity or religion, they may be in a particular socioeconomic class. If you live on what we used to call "the wrong side of the tracks," you're already forced into a faction simply based on where you live. It'll be awfully tough for you to cross the tracks and mingle with the people who are financially and socially much different from your family. If you're Amish or an Orthodox Jew, then at birth, you're in a faction of sorts, one that strongly prefers that you don't marry into another group.

Even being female places you into a faction in our society. You're limited—and I don't care how liberal we are compared to what we were like as a society several decades ago—when you enter traditionally male occupations.

Even within our modern-day factions, we have subfactions. Join any group, go to any high school, and you'll see what I mean.

It's striking how the members of the *Divergent* factions in what Veronica Roth says is based on Chicago are primarily white American-born people. When asked why she chose Chicago as her setting, she says that she lived "next to" Chicago from the age of five, and that she originally wanted to write about the Dauntless riding the Chicago trains.[1] In *Divergent,* where are the immigrants who live in Chicago and the overall United States now? In *Divergent,* where are the minorities, the handicapped, the mentally challenged, and the mentally ill? Where is the prison population?

According to the United States Census Bureau, foreign-born immigrants—that is, people who literally move to the United States from other countries—range from somewhere between 11 million people to 13.8 million people.[2] In addition, experts state that all legal and illegal immigrants plus their children now account for 80 percent of the United States population growth in the past decade, and indeed, immigrants and their children make up one-sixth of the overall population.[3]

Immigrants often are divided (though perhaps not by choice) into what we can think of as factions based on nation, language, and other reasons. Many still speak their foreign languages and don't yet know English. Sadly, many immigrants tend to be much lower on the socioeconomic scale than non-immigrant Americans. This means that many immigrants live apart from non-immigrant Americans, their children attend different schools, their neighborhoods have different customs and codes: in short, many live in different factions, separate from the non-immigrant Americans.

In our modern society, those who are on welfare probably don't associate much with those who live in New York City penthouses. Those who live in poverty in the Deep South aren't hobnobbing with New England socialites. In Chicago, a pocket neighborhood of native-born Chinese probably aren't hanging out with a pocket neighborhood of native-born Peruvians across town.

In fact, let's look specifically at Chicago, where Veronica Roth has set *Divergent* and *Insurgent*. According to the 2010 census, more than 2.5 million people live in Chicago.[4] For those of you who like precision, the number is 2,695,598.

Of this number, 1,212,835 are white people, who seem to dominate the factions in *Divergent* and *Insurgent*. In reality, less than half the people in Chicago are white. In real Chicago, 32 percent of the population is African American, 5½ percent is Asian, close to 29 percent is Hispanic or Latino, and so forth.[5]

While I'm puzzled by the lack of diversity among the people in all of Veronica Roth's factions, I'm also fascinated by the factions themselves, what they mean, and how they interact.

One of the main messages in the trilogy is that people are innately at war with each other; squabbling is something humans just can't seem to live without, and no matter what we do to heal our wounds, cease bickering, and form a more cohesive society, we fail. At the end of *Insurgent,* Amanda Marie Ritter—otherwise known as Edith Prior and Tris's ancestor from seven generations back—shows bloody clips of violence perpetrated by people against their fellow citizens. In *Alle-*

giant, the leader of the Bureau of Genetic Welfare, David, explains that almost half the people in the United States died in the Purity War a hundred years ago. It's human nature, writes Veronica Roth, that makes us violent against each other.[6] In fact, in *Allegiant,* we're told that violence might be rooted in a person's genetic makeup.

Diversity is a big buzzword on college campuses these days, and the Divergent as an offshoot of Veronica Roth's factions are made up of people who are able to understand how other people think and why they act as they do. Supposedly, the minds of the Divergent are more flexible than those in the other factions. But we'll circle back to all of this in a minute.

First, let's talk a bit more about free will, free thought, and freedom versus the notion of factions, in general. Then we'll pick up with brief descriptions and analyses of the various factions in the *Divergent* series.

Why do I want to talk about free will, free thought, and freedom in the context of *Divergent?* Because those who remain in Abnegation believe they are choosing freely to do so, those in Candor do the same, and so forth. Each person as a teenager either stays in his or her birth faction or switches to another faction during a special Choosing Ceremony. This word, *Choosing,* implies that free will, free thought, and freedom are all central to being in the various factions. Most teenagers remain with their family's faction, but some leap off into the strange, new worlds of other factions. Free choice. *Supposedly.*

But is it really free choice? I would argue that very little about these factions involves free will and free choice.

Right off the bat, I'm reminded of both the Aptitude Test and the complex and harrowing initiation stages that Beatrice Prior, aka Tris, completes. First, let's think about the Aptitude

Test that supplies each teenager with an outcome leading to one of the five factions. Of course, if someone is Divergent, then various traits can point to multiple factions. Does this Aptitude Test allow teenagers to use their own free will in determining the faction to which they are most suited? Not really. It's a simulation, which starts when the person chooses between two things, and the choice moves the person to the next step—sort of like a Choose Your Own Adventure book. Well, imagine if you don't want to select either choice. Suppose you're presented with options such as a roasted newborn calf (ugh) and a machine gun (ugh). Now, there's no way I'd choose the roasted newborn calf, and if forced to select, I'd have to go with the machine gun, which might thrust me into the camp of the Dauntless. I am not at all suited to being a Dauntless, and I'd have no freedom of choice in this outcome, would I? Or suppose that you're a very slow learner, perhaps learning disabled, and you must choose rapidly between two things you don't even understand. There's no way you could make a sensible choice, and you (like me in the above example) would have no free will in choosing your faction. Maybe I'd end up Divergent along with my learning-disabled friend. This is somewhat how Tris ends up with the Divergent label: because she first refuses to choose between the first two simulation options, the cheese and the knife.

After this first phase of the simulation, let's say we're presented with something similar to the dog in Tris's Aptitude Test. Perhaps you're a dog lover, who actually trains dogs. Perhaps you're dense and don't understand that this is just a simulation and the dog can't hurt you. Perhaps you're so incredibly terrified of dogs that even knowing this is a simulation, you get hysterical. In this last case, your unconscious mind is taking over and making you terrified. You have no control, no free will, over your lifelong terror of large, growling beasts. Your choice is not truly made with free will.

Our mental states are based on neurotransmissions, neural conditions, interactions among our brain cells. By mental states, I'm referring to such things as desires and beliefs. Without these biological and chemical entities and functions, our mental states cannot exist. We cannot choose anything if these minute processes in our brains cease to function. Over time, as our mental states evolve, neural pathways are emphasized—strengthened by use—or de-emphasized, thus reinforcing the neurotransmissions, neural conditions, and interactions among our brain cells. It's a bit of a circular pattern, this logic, just as the more we do something like play baseball, the better we are at it, which in turn, strengthens our throwing arm or leg muscles. The more we use certain pathways in our brain, the stronger a mental state becomes, strengthening the pathways themselves.

If our desires and beliefs hinge on mental processes that aren't under our constant, minute control, then how can we be held accountable for our actions? Are all of Erudite evil just because Jeanine Matthews is evil? Are all of Dauntless cruel just because some of its members are cruel? I would argue that the individual Erudite and Dauntless are not exercising free will when they follow their leaders, Jeanine and Eric, for if they were operating under free will, they might choose to overthrow their leaders and the entire systems under which they function. Conversely, are Jeanine Matthews and Eric responsible for their horrible behaviors, ideas, and actions, or are their factions responsible because they allow Jeanine and Eric to lead them? Here, I would argue that Jeanine and Eric are indeed operating with free will, because only they can stop leading their factions with such brutality and contempt for human life. Of course, we learn late in *Insurgent* that Dauntless leader Eric is actually an Erudite in disguise.

So within the confines of Chicago for a hundred years before the events of *Divergent,* why don't the people exercise a little free will and overthrow their terrible leaders? I believe it's because they are basically brainwashed into thinking that they have freedom, that whatever faction they are in happens to be the best faction for them. They don't know about the Purity War, they don't know about the genetic manipulations, they don't know what exists outside the fence around Chicago. Even as far into the series as *Allegiant,* Tris points out that Evelyn hasn't liberated the people of Chicago and given them free will. Yes, she destroys the factions, but she also immediately imposes all sorts of new rules and regulations, such as curfews. And without the factions, chaos and violence erupt, and people are killed.

In our culture, in reality, we also think we have free will, and in believing we choose our own destinies, we function in a more moral manner than if we thought we had no control over our own lives. In an interesting 2008 study, psychology professors Kathleen D. Vohs and Jonathan W. Schooler showed that people do indeed act with higher moral standards when they think they are operating with free will.[7] This is similar to factions such as Abnegation, in which people are morally very good, helping the poor, giving rather than taking; the Abnegation believe they have chosen their faction and their way of life, and hence, they act in a moral fashion. The Abnegation represents our moral code as in "do unto others as you'd like them to do unto you" and "help other people at all times." These ideas are ground into our major Western religions and charities, and into youth groups such as the Scouts. If they did not choose Abnegation, if instead they were forced into the faction, then would they be so morally uprighteous? Probably not.

Similarly, if they realized the constraints upon them as faction members, they might be a bit resentful and not so selfless. After all, if you know that you don't have the free will to do what you want, you also know that your efforts to change things will most likely be futile. Poor Al wants to fit into the Dauntless and appear tough when he's not at all tough. He'd be a lot better off if he could realize that he can't change anything, that even being Factionless would beat what happens to him in Dauntless. "Choosing" to switch from Candor, Al's honesty in saying that he's afraid gets him into trouble with Eric during the knife-throwing scene. The Divergent Tris, on the other hand, who does exercise free will to determine her fate and her actions, steps in and takes Al's place as the knife target. She displays the bravado of Dauntless and the selflessness of Abnegation. Also, when she tells Eric that bullies are cowards, she's being not only Dauntless brave, but Erudite smart as well. She outwits Eric at his own idiotic bullying game. All he can do is prod her into taking Al's place. Tobias, aka Four, who is presumed Divergent until the events in *Allegiant,* displays Dauntless bravery, selfless Abnegation, and Erudite knowledge, too, because he's the guy who is going to throw the knives at Tris. Four purposely nicks Tris's ear and insults her while throwing knives at her. This is all a ruse to make Eric think he's still really in control; but he's not. While Four supposedly has gene damage, he also has genetic "components" that enable him to know what he's doing during the simulations. So he is Divergent-like.

The factions exist to separate people into groups, just as factions naturally exist in real life that separate people into groups. The difference is that the factions in the Divergent series are artificially created by people. In the *Allegiant*, Veronica Roth tells us who has created these factions and exactly why. After reading the first two books, all we know is that Amanda Ritter, aka Edith Prior, represents the group who created the factions, that this group saw people as too immoral and violent, and hence separated people in hopes that the Divergent population with their flexible minds would grow.

While we all think we're individuals, we're also part of groups or factions. We need groups to feel that we belong. If we correlate people as members of groups, it colors our response to and our interactions with those people. For example, Peter calls all Dauntless by the name Stiff. Tris is surprised that her mother acts like a Dauntless instead of an Abnegation. She's surprised by her brother Caleb's Erudite behavior because he was always the one who exhibited the more pronounced Abnegation traits. Nobody would expect an Amity to burn down a forest or an Abnegation to steal from the poor. Even when the factions collapse, Tris still feels the urge to group people. She keeps putting people into faction categories simply out of habit. Evelyn states it bluntly on page 20 of *Allegiant*, that "people always organize into groups. That's a fact of our existence."

Sadly, as the Divergent series's factions learn, dividing and separating people doesn't work very well in the long run. It creates an "us versus them" attitude. It's dangerous. When you place yourself into a group, then simply by defining the group's characteristics and traits, by thinking of your group as "us," you are by extension defining everyone else as not in your group, as "them." This creates misunderstandings and tension. It creates prejudices, bigotry, and war.

Groups encourage people to be with others who think the

same way and can have a huge impact on behaviors and thoughts. By balancing the pros and cons of group membership, a person may go to great lengths to escape commitment to one group and to join another group. This is what Tris does in *Divergent* when she leaves Abnegation for Dauntless. She must leave behind her family to make this move from one group to another. And on Visiting Day, families don't necessarily visit those they consider traitors, those who left their faction for another. Is this any different from the Amish "Forsaken," who are banned by their own families if they leave the Amish way to join other groups of people? The motto Faction Before Blood is taken quite seriously. As early as page 43 of *Divergent,* Tris is already questioning her allegiance to factions; she already wonders if it's a good thing that factions, groups, define who and what everyone is rather than families.

A MINI-LOOK AT TRIS PRIOR

As the main character in the Divergent series, Tris must overcome her self-doubts and weaknesses in order to remain alive. However, her toughness and determination far exceed her need simply to survive. They show that Tris wants to succeed at all costs to herself, that she doesn't want to give up the battle, and that she has an underlying need to prove to the other Dauntless that she's the best. Do you think she does all this because she wants to be accepted or popular in some way? It doesn't quite feel that this is the case, does it? It's clear that she wants to fit in with the born-Dauntless and to be taken seriously, but as for being popular, she doesn't seem at all interested in joining established power cliques, such as the one led by Candor-born Peter. And while she does want to be the best, Tris doesn't want to formally lead the Dauntless.

She wants their approval and she wants to win, but she doesn't want the mantle of responsibility that comes with being a leader. This ultimately frees her from the evil that is centered in the current Dauntless leadership.

When Beatrice Prior leaves her family's faction, the Abnegation, to join the Dauntless, she changes her name to Tris. This shows that she wants to go down the Dauntless path as a new person, as if she's starting her life all over again. The tattoos and new clothing also mark the beginning of her new persona as a Dauntless. Sometimes, when we need to turn our backs on people and things that matter a lot to us, we have to make the cuts in ways that enable us to move forward without falling apart. A complete cut with the past can squelch weakness and any feelings of regret. Most likely, when Beatrice changes her name, her clothes, her attitude, and gets the tattoos, she's removing herself as far as she can from her former faction and life. People often dress a certain way to "fit in," and they adopt modes of communication and physical stances to fit in with groups they want to join. In real life, people who have a lot of self-confidence may ignore these tendencies and simply dress, talk, and behave in their own manners. But when fitting in is essential to survival, either in Tris's case or in real-life scenarios—for example, in a corporate business environment, a woman wearing a bikini isn't going to get past the front door—people do what they think is necessary.

Tris continually agitates about whether Tobias/Four takes her seriously enough. She clearly loves him and wants to be with him. It's difficult, of course, to even have a *first date*. They almost break up during *Allegiant*. By the end of the book, she dies, and still, he misses her. Had she lived, it's possible their relationship would have endured and blossomed.

According to Marcus on page 42 of *Divergent*, each "man" has the "right to choose his own way in this world." However, he's not speaking the truth, because each person actually has the right to choose to belong to one of only five specific factions. This is not really free will. In addition, the only faction that allows a person to think on multiple planes, the Divergent, is basically considered dangerous to the well-being of the overall population.

Most people in the real world would probably be more like the Divergent than any of the other factions. How many of us are always selfless—in other words, similar to the Abnegation? How many of us are always, 100 percent of the time, kind and loving—in other words, similar to the Amity? How many of us are always honest, no matter what the consequences—similar to the Candor? How many of us are always buried in our books, researching everything in minute detail, cold and calculating, with little warmth toward even our own families—as with the Erudite? And how many of us are always aggressively brave to the point of brutality, bullying, and near-suicidal acts, as in jumping off the tallest buildings in Chicago—as with the Dauntless? If you think about yourself, your friends and family, basically everyone you know, you'll probably find that most of us are sometimes selfless, sometimes kind and loving, sometimes honest, sometimes intellectual and coldly logical, and sometimes aggressive and brave. Each person combines all these traits, as well as many others. So I believe that most of us would actually fall into the Divergent category.

The only current factions that could cause trouble for the others might be Dauntless and Erudite because all the other factions focus on meeker traits such as selflessness, honesty, and loving-kindness. So the system seems set up for pitting faction against faction, which is probably a big reason why it's wise to isolate the factions from one another. I don't, by the way, agree with Tris's father, who says that people who crave knowledge wind up lusting for power. This isn't necessarily true at all. If it were, every major scientist would be a power-hungry control freak, whereas most scientists are seeking to discover truths, simple as that. (I feel qualified to state this—with the caveat that it is my opinion—because I live with several scientists and know dozens more.)

Even in the *Divergent* world's high school, kids of different factions avoid each other and only mix in oddball places, such as a hallway cast in light. Each faction dresses in a specific way, as do the Amish and the Hasidim in our society. This serves to keep factions separate from one another. They have different customs, mores, and manners.

Some factions allow children to play openly. Others require that children keep to themselves, pray a lot, and help around the house.

Even with all the separate customs and isolation, people in the same faction don't always get along. This is certainly true in the real world, as well. On page 81 of *Divergent,* Will tells Christina and Tris that "just because we're in the same faction doesn't mean we get along." He's explaining why he's not hanging out with other former members of Erudite. And rife within the books are squabbles and infighting among the members of Dauntless, as seen through Tris's eyes. Peter and his posse, Drew and Molly, are like mean bullies, and even some of the leaders of Dauntless are mean as sin. When Tris does well, she has to step cautiously because she knows other initiates may be jealous of her bravery and progress.

A MINI-LOOK AT PETER

The Amity-born Peter is a Dauntless initiate who likes to bully people, especially Tris. At some point in life, everyone has been subjected to the taunts and bullying of a person like Peter. He tries to get under Tris's skin by calling her names such as Stiff, which refers to the fact that she's from Abnegation, where people rigidly remain selfless and live in a world of gray. He and his little gang of bullies rip off her towel and then he makes fun of her naked body, which is about as humiliating as you can get! But he's much more than a name-calling bully, isn't he?

He's *dangerous*. For example, during the Dauntless initiation process, he stabs Edward in the eye with a knife. As another example, he attacks Tris, wraps his hand around her throat, and then almost throws her into the chasm, where Al died. He becomes enraged simply by the fact that after stage two, Tris ranks first and he ranks second.

Despite everything he says and, worse, does to Tris, when he's supposed to inject her with a death serum, he doesn't do it. Even Tris is confused by his behavior. It is very strange behavior for a bully who beats people up and doesn't mind choking them and tossing them into chasms to suddenly save an enemy's life. He explains it away by saying he couldn't stand the thought of owing her anything, but if she's dead, why would this matter to him? So Tris had saved his life by shoving him out of the way of a bullet. Peter doesn't strike me as the type who would repay the kindness by saving her life in return.

According to Peter, people do things either because they want something in return or because they owe you something. This isn't always the case, however. People do kind things simply because it's the right thing to do. They empathize with others. They feel the pain of others. They want to make other people happy. There are a lot of other reasons for doing things that go well beyond petty selfishness or keeping score.

In an interesting turn of events, Peter changes in character by the end of *Allegiant*. He's tired of being a bully and wants to make a fresh start. The assumption here is that people are violent based largely on genetics, so Peter's bullying might be caused by his genetic makeup. He can't help himself, or so we might think, given the information provided in *Allegiant*. Mere therapy won't work. The only thing that Peter can do, he figures, is swill a vial of the memory-erasure serum. This way, he won't be the same Peter anymore.

I'm not sure how this might work. If indeed Peter's bad personality is based on genetics, then erasing his memory won't heal him and turn him into a generous, loving, kind person. If his bad personality is based on his upbringing and his environment, then erasing his memory might help change him.

Would you create additional factions if you were organizing the society in the *Divergent* series? Selflessness, honesty, knowledge, peace and loving-kindness, and bravery: these are represented in the current factions.

I would argue that the word *trustworthy* has a different meaning from the word *honest*. If I trust a friend not to divulge a private and confidential secret, and if that friend is a member of Candor, then she's going to divulge my secret and betray my confidence—she can't help herself, she's Candor and always tells the truth, regardless of the consequences. Perhaps the idea of being trustworthy should be melded into the Candor honesty code.

What about loyalty? The entire faction system is set up to

make sure people are loyal to the factions rather than to individual people. Would you really want to live this way? I wouldn't. My loyalties are cemented in notions such as family and friends, and it's people, individuals, who come before any groups with which I identify. If you're in a club at school and somebody verbally attacks your best friend and calls him vulgar, race-related names, you'll stand up and defend your friend, even if it means quitting the overall club. So I believe the critical element of "loyalty to individuals" is missing from the factions in *Divergent*.

What happens with religions within the various factions? Certainly in Candor, if a person disagrees with the religious beliefs of another person, bickering and possible violence could occur. We have enough trouble with this issue in our real world, where many times, people are smart enough to keep their mouths shut when they disagree with somebody else's religious beliefs. As David puts it in *Allegiant*, the Candor might be honest, but they're also inconsiderate. In Dauntless, if someone is a bigot or racist of any kind, watch out: he could be dangerous. If you have any religious faith in Erudite, you'd better keep it to yourself because the cold, calculating logic and vanity of the Erudite may not allow for specific forms of religious behavior or even touchy-feely things such as belief in God.

Would you create a religious- and racial/ethnic-compassion faction? It could serve as a haven to those who have been subjected to religious and racial/ethnic abuse.

Would you create a faction for the felons, the murderers, thieves, pedophiles, and the like? Where are they in the *Divergent* society? We don't know.

And what about the mentally slow and handicapped? We don't know where they are, either, in the *Divergent* world. Would you isolate them into a separate faction or allow them to stay with their families' factions? It would be difficult for certain people to make it through the Aptitude Test, much less the initiations, in order to make the choice to switch factions. If you limit these people, then aren't you taking away their freedom to choose, their free will?

Similarly, we don't know anything about the physically disabled in this world. Where are they? And where are the hospitalized people? Do the various factions intermingle within hospitals, or are they confined to faction-specific hospitals? Where do they die, where are they buried: in faction-specific cemeteries?

In essence, the society of *Divergent* forces individuals into groups, which means the people actually have no civil liberties and freedom to live where they want and do what they want. It dehumanizes everybody by forcing people to conform to strict codes of conduct and dress and even thought. How different is this from George Orwell's classic novel *1984* (Secker and Warburg, 1949)? Big Brother is a figurehead of the Party, and while he may be a real person, he may just be a symbol. What he symbolizes is the collapse of civil liberties and rights, the dehumanization of people, and thought control. As portrayed in *1984*, we're heading toward a global war, and after that war, three super-states will divide up all the land and then control everyone in their provinces. Hence, as with the factions in the world of *Divergent*, the novel *1984* used three factions, or super-states—slightly different methods of carving up people into factions, but in essence, the same overall idea. Divide the people, control what they do and say, and hope that this method keeps the peace. In *1984*, the citizens are so dehumanized, they're known as "unpersons." Things aren't quite this extreme in *Divergent*, where people are led to believe that they are choosing their own paths using free will. In *1984,* if Winston Smith is caught "thinking" rebellious ideas, he can be executed. Again, things aren't quite this extreme in *Divergent;* although if you consider what happens to Al at the hands of his own faction, the Dauntless, perhaps those who think rebellious ideas specific to their factions fall to the same fates as the rebellious in *1984.*

In *1984,* the government controls the people's view of reality in order to control the people. Nobody in *1984* really knows what's going on around the world.

Things are not much different in *Divergent,* where nobody knows why the factions are locked out of the rest of the world at the gate. Who is the master planner behind the factions, the Divergent, the overall scheme of life? We don't know even at the end of *Insurgent,* though we finally get answers to all our questions in the third novel, *Allegiant.* In fact, a major theme in *Allegiant* is that Tris needs to find out what's happening beyond the fence that confines people to what used to be Chicago.

Aldous Huxley's *Brave New World* and Ray Bradbury's *Fahrenheit 451* both differ somewhat from *1984.* Both show the oppressive results of brainwashing, blind faith in the government and technology, and a conscious reduction by the government in the intellectual and individual liberties of citizens.

These ideas are present in the *Divergent* series, as well: people are essentially brainwashed into thinking their factions make the most sense; they have blind faith and function like robots, really, staying in their factions, rigidly adhering to the minutia of rules; and they don't know it, but they have very little in the way of intellectual and individual liberties.

Brave New World, of course, gives us a world state with

extremely stultifying social stability but without any war . . . yet. In *1984* and *Fahrenheit 451*, people fear enemy attacks and war, with torture and deprivation commonplace.

In *Divergent*, the factions evolve after much violence among the people. There's been no outright war specifically in the first two novels, not yet, but at the end of *Insurgent*, we feel something's brewing, and it's not going to be pleasant.

During *Allegiant*, we learn about the Purity War that occurred some one hundred years ago. This war was similar to what we see in books such as *1984*, *Fahrenheit 451*, and *The Hunger Games*. Fought between the genetically damaged and the genetically pure, the Purity War wiped out half the population of the United States. The government, just as in the other books I just mentioned, instituted severe control measures to avoid additional violence and death.

As in *The Hunger Games*, most people in the Divergent series don't really know what's going on. Nita explicitly tells Tris in *Allegiant* that people are "isolated, starving," and in addition, are under the control of government propaganda. As in *The Hunger Games*, the government has been lying to everybody about their history.

If you count what kids go through during initiation, you might say that torture is commonplace in *Divergent*. If I had to jump off moving trains and Ferris wheels and tall buildings, I'd think of it as torture. If someone forced me to teeter on a rail with certain death should I fall, I'd consider it torture and brutality. It's a fine line, isn't it?

No society is going to work when people are more committed to the "state" than to one another. Societies tend to break down under these conditions. We need only look at repressive states such as Stalin's so-called socialist regime, which massacred and imprisoned millions of its own citizens.

I would suggest that by the end of *Insurgent*, with the factions already at war, the *Divergent* world's society has indeed splintered and broken down. There may not be a Stalin or a symbolic Big Brother at the head of the government, but somebody's pulling the strings. Although the government is run by people in Abnegation, we know by the end of *Insurgent* that there are forces greater than the known government. Also, we know that people in the other factions greatly resent being governed by Abnegation.

People can be repressed for just so long before they revolt and war breaks out. Perhaps the insanity unleashed by Jeanine Matthews is the trigger. Perhaps she is the Stalin figure, who seeks to control all the other factions. For example, Jack Kang at Candor headquarters tells everybody that Jeanine Matthews has told him via her representative that the Candor are weak and depend on Erudite for their very survival, that Kang must do what she wants or his faction will no longer be "free." (page 268, *Insurgent*)

Also, why do you think most of the Divergent come from Abnegation rather than the other factions? It might be because it's necessary to be selfless in order to see things from other people's viewpoints. It's the Abnegation, after all, who take care of the poor and needy and the Factionless in this society. They must have a lot of empathy in their natures. If you count the Factionless as a legitimate group, then there are actually more Divergent in the Factionless than in Abnegation.

Here's a quick summary of the various factions:

Abnegation = Selfless, although we can also think of them as repressed. Are they truly capable of friendship when they can't accept favors and acts of kindness? Are they truly happy when they never laugh aloud and get a little crazy? Is it healthy to bottle up all your own desires, needs, and emotions?

Amity = Happy, peaceful, loving. On the flip side, they can't handle conflicts, and they can't do anything by force or persuasion. Because they must cooperate at all times, how are they capable of loyalty? Think about Johanna's disloyalty in telling the Erudite and Dauntless that the Abnegation, former Erudite initiates, and three Dauntless are hiding in the Amity compound. The Amity can't bring themselves to vocalize objections to a search for the very people they're hiding.

Candor = Honest, see the world as black-and-white with no room for anything in between, argues too much. On their flip side, they don't sound particularly tolerant. People can look at the same thing with different perceptions and reactions. People aren't always just right or wrong. People have different opinions, modes of behavior, and dress. Who's to say, really, that only the extremes are valid?

Erudite = Intelligent, seek knowledge at all costs. Of course, we know that the Erudite get out of control, they become absurdly arrogant and power hungry, they attack Tris's father and all the Abnegation, they cause strife and violence.

Dauntless = Brave. Their flip side is that they take too many risks, they become bullies, and their dangerous lives cause people to die. It seems there are no old Dauntless, for as Tobias says, as soon as a Dauntless person becomes physically incapable of continuing, the faction ousts him.

Allegiant = Faction loyalist, maybe afraid of change. The Allegiant want to overthrow all the Factionless as well as Evelyn, and they want to reestablish the factions. Because the Allegiant aren't a faction inside Chicago, they aren't part of the Aptitude Tests.

Now you have everything you need to take your own Aptitude Test. Let's give it a whirl.

YOUR APTITUDE TEST

We can't quite put you into a virtual reality immersion or any other form of simulated environment within the pages of this book. Nor can we inject you with serums and stick electrodes on your skin. But we can play a little game, in which you try to determine which faction best suits you. Pretend for a moment that you live in Tris's world, that you're sixteen years old, and that you must undergo an **Aptitude Test** and a **Choosing Ceremony**. You must choose your own faction. Let's see how well you do.

Question 1. You cut your own hair without using a mirror. You wear nothing but drab, gray clothes. You live in a gray house. You eat gray food. You're not even sure what you look like. All of this pleases you, and you wouldn't want it any other way. When somebody suggests that you go wild and wear ripped jeans and a T-shirt and maybe get a real haircut in a shop with mirrors, what do you do?

A. Refuse. Gray is the new every-color, and you won't budge. You see no point in cutting your hair in any way other than how you've always hacked it off with your mother's nail scissors. And besides, you don't want to know what you look like. So you shy away from the person who is suggesting these dramatic changes in you. You fade into the shadows. You walk away.

B. You answer that gray is drab, that ripped jeans are too common, that the T-shirt looks too tight. As for your hair, you admit it could be better, but then again, the person suggesting all these changes to you has hair the color and shape of a monkey's. You suggest that the person lose weight and wear better-fitting clothes.

C. You respond that you have no interest in creature comforts, that clothing and hair are irrelevant to you. Later, you visit a tattoo parlor, get a nose ring, and have your hair done into an array of pink and green spikes. When the person who made the ludicrous suggestions to you shows up again and is stunned by your appearance, you spit on the ground and growl, "Yeah, what of it?"

D. You respond that the person's suggestions are extremely kind and generous. You tell the person that you love him and everything about him. You hold his hand. You sing "Kum-baya."

E. You study every issue of *Vogue* magazine since its first issue in 1892. You analyze what works on your body shape and size. You study hair design at the finest couture boutiques. You study architecture and interior design. Then and only then, you decide on the best course of action regarding your hair, living environment, and clothing.

Question 2. Your school closes for an entire week in the summer. Your parents are out of town but gave you access to money, cars, and anything else you could possibly want. Yes, let's pretend that you're *this* wealthy and *this* lucky. What do you do with your week of freedom?

A. You invite all your friends to join you at the top of the Empire State Building. Then you tie everyone to bungee cords, and you all jump off. The next day, you get everyone to take a long Amtrak ride and force them to jump off as the train soars over cliffs and beneath tight overhangs. What fun! You follow every excursion with a little midnight paintball.

B. You tell your parents up front that you will most likely spend all their money and wreck their cars, that they really shouldn't leave teenagers alone at home for a week at a time.

C. You plant flowers, bake cakes, sing show tunes and biblical hymns, and paint peace signs on the sidewalk.

D. You study twenty hours every day for next week's schoolwork.

E. You give all your parents' money and cars to the poor. You sell their house and give the proceeds to charity. You sell their clothes. You check into a bleak hotel at the edge of town.

Question 3. A family member always treats you badly. At every family gathering, she shows up at your house, then proceeds to ignore you completely or manipulate you. Sometimes, she reduces you to tears, and she's even spied on you and stolen things from you. This year, she shows up yet again for another family gathering at your house. How do you react?

A. You consider beating in her face, but resist the urge. Instead, you defend your baby sister, Emma, from the bullying.

B. You tell her that you can't stand her, that she's a despicable pest and needs to wise up and grow up.

C. You act as if she's never offended you in the past. You welcome her into your home and treat her the same as you treat every other member of your family.

D. You tell she's ignorant and give her all the tomes ever written by experts about philosophy, ethics, morals, and relationships.

E. You say nothing to her. When she insults you, you simply pass a tray of cookies her way. When she ignores you, you talk to somebody else. When she makes fun of your face, you smile, knowing that physical appearances are irrelevant.

Question 4. Eight huge thugs are beating up a little boy and his puppy. You're only four feet eight inches tall, and you weight seventy-five pounds. What do you do?

A. You've studied physics and calculus at the graduate level. You know exactly how much force to apply and at what angles you must hold your fists and arms. You know how to throw a peanut with incredible impact, a force sufficient enough to blind a man. You enter the battle, knowing exactly how to win.

B. You tell the thugs, "Take me instead of the boy and puppy. Take me." You spread your arms and gaze toward the heavens. You wait for the assault, happy in the knowledge that the boy can grab his puppy and run free.

C. You jump into the battle and flail away with all your might to save the little boy and his puppy. You're scrappier than you gave yourself credit for, as you leap from tree limbs and kick the brutes in their faces. Your brass knuckles do wonders. The bullies shouldn't have messed with those who are too young and weak to defend themselves. The puppy snuggles in your arms, and the boy cries.

D. You tell the thugs that they don't really want to hurt anybody, do they? You tell them that, if they let the boy and puppy go, you'll take them to your house for a good game of croquet and a snack of apple pie and juice. You tell them that God will forgive them.

E. You tell the brutes that they belong in jail and should be ashamed of themselves. You tell the little boy that he shouldn't be out this time of night, alone in a strange neighborhood, much less with a puppy.

Question 5. You're in high school, and the SATs are coming up. All your friends are talking about the colleges where they want to go, and why. What are you thinking?

A. You probably won't bother taking the SATs or applying to college. You intend to devote your life to acts of charity, perhaps continuing your work in the soup kitchen and homeless shelter.

B. The SATs don't matter much to you, and you also don't care where you attend college. Perhaps the local community college will work best for you, and you can get an associate's degree in psychology or art. Or perhaps you'll just forgo all that college stuff and play your guitar on the streets and in clubs for small wages. Or perhaps you'll head out West and work on a pony farm. You don't really know what you want to do, but as long as you're giddy with joy and spreading the love, who cares?

C. You're not afraid of those flippin' SATs. You know that you'll get into a good college no matter how well you do on the tests. You'll get in anywhere you want to go simply because you tend to get what you want. You know how to get things done.

D. You tell your friends the truth, that some of them shouldn't go to college because they're not smart enough to succeed. You tell other friends to get jobs at McDonald's rather than take the SATs and apply to college. You analyze your own possibility for good scores on the SATs. You realize it's hopeless, that no matter how much you study, you'll never achieve scores high enough to get into a top college. You admit your weaknesses to your friends, and although they try to cheer you up, you shake your head and tell them that it's all fine, that you know your place in the world, and if you're destined for a mediocre score, then so be it. Knowing the truth is better than pretending you're something that you're not.

E. You race to the library and take out all the SAT study guides. You buy every study guide available online. You hole up for six months, making sure you can answer every question correctly, not only on the standard Verbal and Mathematics SATs, but also on the Reading SAT and all the Achievement SATs for Physics, Chemistry, Biology, Mathematics, and so on. It's not so much that you need to go to Harvard to feel good about yourself. No, no, it's that you need to know everything possible to feel good about yourself.

Question 6. You would rather be known as:

A. Intellectually brilliant instead of sweet and kind

B. Someone people can trust in any situation

C. Someone who will fight for them at all costs to yourself

D. Sweet and kind rather than intellectually brilliant

E. Someone who will give people the shirt off your own back.

Question 7. Your parents move to a new city, and you have to go to a new high school in tenth grade. This is your big chance to change your entire persona. You've always wanted to be part of the in crowd. The only question is: Which in crowd is it?

A. At long last, you can be the person you truly believe you are. No longer do you have to wear prissy skirts and button-down shirts. No longer do you have to wear ponytails. You go to school on the first day wearing black leather pants and a ripped death metal T-shirt. You shave your head and dye the stubble orange. Instead of sitting with all the normal kids up front and in the middle of the room, you gravitate to the back, where all the tough kids are sneering at the teacher. They're talking about motorcycles and graffiti. You can't wait to join them.

B. At long last, you can be the person you truly believe you are. No longer do you have to wear filthy jeans and your brother's old shirts. No longer do you have to wear heavy black eye makeup and sport twelve piercings on your lips. Instead of sitting in the back of the room with all the punks, you sit up front with all the smart kids. You wear a prissy skirt and a button-down shirt. Your hair is in a ponytail. You raise your hand, hoping the teacher calls on you, because you always know the correct answer to every question.

C. At long last, you can be the person you truly believe you are. No longer do you have to pretend that you fit in anywhere. You tell the punks in the back of the room that they should stop sneering at the teacher, listen to what she says, wise up, and pay attention. You tell the smart, prissy kids that they need to lighten up, live a little, smell the roses, have some fun. Everybody glares at you, and you can tell that the punks want to bash your face in. You don't mind, not really. You're just telling it the way it is.

D. At long last, you can be the person you truly believe you are. You don't have to wear prissy skirts and button-down shirts. You don't have to wear ponytails. You don't have to wear black leather pants and a ripped death metal T-shirt. You don't have to shave your head and dye the stubble orange. You don't have to wear filthy jeans and your brother's old shirts. It doesn't matter what you wear or what you look like, not anymore. You sit with all the wallflowers and the kid who talks about his toy trains and his stuffed bear. You sit with the girl wearing the 1950s ill-fitting dress that her grandmother gave to her. You sit with the kid who dresses up as a garbage bag for Halloween. You'd be content wearing that garbage bag, wouldn't you? Anything will do. You're comfortable in your gray overalls. You fade into the walls. You feel just fine. In the girls' locker room later, some kid makes fun of your overalls. You smile, take off your overalls, and give them to the girl wearing her grandmother's ill-fitting dress. She's happy, you're wearing only your gray underwear, and you feel just fine. You know that your own sister is so selfless that she'll give you the gray shirt off her own gray back, but you know that you won't be able to bring yourself to take it, right? The gym teacher gives you a soiled robe to wear home. It used to be white, but it's been washed so many times with dark colors that it's more like a gray robe now, one with holes and blotches and food stains on it. This works just fine for you. It makes you abundantly happy to see the girl walk out of school wearing your overalls. This is the way it's supposed to be.

E. At long last, you can be the person you truly believe you are. You get along with everybody. You smile at the punks, and they smile back. You smile at the prissy clique girls, and they smile back. You smile at the jocks, the theater crew, the cheerleaders, the brainiacs, and they all smile back at you. It doesn't really matter what you wear or where you sit in the classroom. You love everyone, and everyone loves you, and this is the way it's supposed to be.

Question 8. Quite often, people tell you that you're insensitive. If a friend is wearing an ugly outfit, you tell her. If someone's acne is particularly obscene one day, you have no problem pointing it out. If questioned about your private life, you can't help but tell the truth, even if hurts other people and exposes your most intimate secrets. It is clear that you belong in which faction?

A. Abnegation
B. Amity
C. Candor
D. Dauntless
E. Erudite

Question 9. You want to be elected the leader of your faction. On what do you base your qualifications?

A. You promise to serve everyone with no thought about your own needs.
B. You believe in happiness, kindness, peace, and love for everybody.
C. You promise to always tell the truth to your people.
D. You emphasize that you're tough, resolute, and bold, that your character is very strong.
E. You know all the facts about every issue your people confront.

Question 10. You're terrified of dogs, and the only place to take a walk where you live is around a deserted neighborhood where the dogs run loose. You've been bitten by dogs numerous times. They've chased you, growling and biting at your socks. But you're dying to get out of the house and take a walk. There's nobody to go with you. So what do you do?

A. You've studied twenty-five dog-training manuals, and you already know how to handle the situation.

B. You trust that the dogs won't hurt you. You believe that all creatures love one another, and you've worked hard to love dogs, even ones that weigh twice as much as you do. With love in your heart, you take your walk with the dogs.

C. You've walked the dogs of all the people who live in the deserted neighborhood. Hence, all these dogs already know you, and you feel comfortable that they won't attack you.

D. You've already told the dog owners that their animals are malicious pests that chase, bite, and terrify people. You go for the walk, and when a dog bites your ankle, you grab him by the collar and haul him up to a house, where you knock on the door, then toss the dog inside and yell at the owners that their animals are way out of control.

E. You go alone for your walk. Terrified, yes, but when the dogs chase you, you don't run. Instead, you stand still and keep your voice calm, and you try to control your racing heart. When a dog bites your ankle, you wrench free and still try to remain calm. You pretend you're a dog owner, and you know how to talk to naughty dogs who bite people.

And now, let's take a look at the results of your Aptitude Test.

Question 1.

If you chose A, give yourself one point for Abnegation.

If you chose B, give yourself one point for Candor.

If C, one point for Dauntless.

If D, one point for Amity.

If E, one point for Erudite.

Question 2.

If you chose A, give yourself one point for Dauntless.

If you chose B, give yourself one point for Candor.

If C, one point for Amity.

If D, one point for Erudite.

If E, one point for Abnegation.

Question 3.

If you chose A, give yourself one point for Dauntless.

If you chose B, give yourself one point for Candor.

If C, one point for Amity.

If D, one point for Erudite.

If E, one point for Abnegation.

Question 4.

If you chose A, give yourself one point for Erudite.

If you chose B, give yourself one point for Abnegation.

If C, one point for Dauntless.

If D, one point for Amity.

If E, one point for Candor.

Question 5.

If you chose A, give yourself one point for Abnegation.

If you chose B, give yourself one point for Amity.

If C, one point for Dauntless.

If D, one point for Candor.

If E, one point for Erudite.

Question 6.

If you chose A, give yourself one point for Erudite.

If you chose B, give yourself one point for Candor.

If C, one point for Dauntless.

If D, one point for Amity.

If E, one point for Abnegation.

Question 7.

If you chose A, give yourself one point for Dauntless.

If you chose B, give yourself one point for Erudite.

If C, one point for Candor.

If D, one point for Abnegation.

If E, one point for Amity.

Question 8.

If you chose C, give yourself one point for Candor.

For any other answer, give yourself zero points for all factions.

Question 9.

If you chose A, give yourself one point for Abnegation.

If you chose B, give yourself one point for Amity.

If C, one point for Candor.

If D, one point for Dauntless.

If E, one point for Erudite.

Question 10.

If you chose A, give yourself one point for Erudite.

If you chose B, give yourself one point for Amity.

If C, one point for Abnegation.

If D, one point for Candor.

If E, one point for Dauntless.

It's easy to tally your points. If you received more points for Abnegation than any of the other factions, then this is the faction for which you have the most aptitude. The same is true for the other factions, so if, for example, you received more points for Candor than the other factions, then you probably show the most aptitude for Candor.

NEUROSCIENCE AND GENETICS OF THE FACTIONS

Much of what happens in the Divergent series is based on modern neuroscience and futuristic extensions of current research. Before examining how serums, transmitters, and simulations might affect people in the various factions, it makes sense to understand a little about the minds of people who believe primarily in selflessness, love and peace, brute honesty, bravery in the face of anything, and the pursuit of knowledge at all costs. There's an actual field of study called psychobiology, which attempts to examine our behaviors based on the biology of our brains and bodies.

This will be a brief examination, provided simply to give you an underpinning of what's real in the Divergent series. Bear with me because it'll make everything clearer to you when I talk about the serums and transmitters in later chapters. To understand what Veronica Roth is talking about when she explains that the Divergent have more mirror neurons that most people, you need to know something about neurons. To understand how the serums and transmitters might work, you need to know something about overall brain chemistry.

The brain, spinal cord, and nerves in our bodies contain cells called neurons, and in addition, the brain contains other cells called the glia. While the neurons transmit signals throughout our bodies and brains, the glia support the neurons. Whenever you feel or think something, whenever anything changes in your environment and triggers your senses in any way, millions of neurons fire messages back and forth. These messages consist of electrical impulses and neurotransmissions, or chemicals.

Each neuron, as you probably remember from school, connects to other neurons using branches called dendrites and axons. One neuron may have thousands of these branches. The dendrites bring messages into the neurons, while the axons, which can actually be up to four feet long, transmit messages from the neurons. Between each dendrite and axon in a neural pathway is a tiny space, about one-millionth of an inch, called a synaptic cleft. On the side of the axon, which transmits messages, is a larger presynaptic area; and on the side of the dendrite, which receives messages, is a larger postsynaptic area. Together, the synaptic cleft, presynaptic area, and postsynaptic area are termed the synapse.

Chemicals called neurotransmitters travel across the

synapses linking each axon and dendrite. The neurotransmitters come in many types—possibly hundreds—and the neurons manufacture them using the amino acids in our food.

The neurons not only make the neurotransmitters, but they also store them in areas called vesicles, which are near the ends of the axons. Neurons manufacture some neurotransmitters in the body of the neurons and then ship them off for storage in the vesicles, and they manufacture other neurotransmitters directly in the vesicles.

Of particular interest to any discussion about *Divergent* is the fact that you can inject neurotransmitters into specific parts of the brain and simulate what happens if the neurotransmissions occur naturally. In other words, injected neurotransmissions basically can do the same things as natural neurotransmissions. This is probably how the serums and transmitters function on a very basic level, and we'll delve into these topics later in this book.

When it's not transmitting information, a neuron is at rest and its axons have more negative ions—chemicals with electric charge—than exist outside it. This means the axon has a negative charge, and the fluid outside it has a positive charge.

When the neuron gets excited, positively charged sodium ions enter the axon, depolarizing it and turning the inner charge positive. The change in electric charge rips all the way from one end of the axon to the other, creating what is called an action potential, or electrical impulse, which in turn, prompts the vesicles to zip to the axon and release neurotransmitters into the synaptic cleft.

As the vesicles release the neurotransmitters, positively charged potassium ions gush from the axon, hence restoring the axon's negative charge.

At this point, the neuron is at rest again.

Meantime, the neurotransmitters travel across the synaptic cleft and reach the dendrites of other connected neurons. If the other neuron's dendrite has receptors that are genetically designed to receive these specific neurotransmitters, then the neurotransmitters bind to the receptors. A receptor is actually a protein that enables a neurotransmitter to connect to a dendrite.

In the case of *Divergent,* if a neurotransmitter in a serum or injection is designed to bind to specific receptors, then that neurotransmitter can indeed alter the brain's functions.

As you might have guessed, the receptor itself transforms when it binds to the neurotransmitter. It basically opens the gateway into the other neuron and lets ions flow into it. These ions either depolarize the other neuron—that is, make its inner charge positive to match the positively charged outer fluid—or polarize it—that is, make its inner charge negative to be the opposite of the positively charged outer fluid. In addition, the transformation of the receptor activates specific proteins. The basic concept to remember is that each receptor operates like a gateway or security door, accepting only specific neurotransmitters as if they were passwords specific to the neuron.

Following the binding process, the receptor releases the neurotransmitter, and at this point, a couple of things can happen. For one, proteins might carry the neurotransmitter back to its originating axon in what is called the reuptake process. It's not so much a rejection of the neurotransmitter as a way of enabling the originating neuron to use the neurotransmitter again. For another, enzymes might step in and destroy the neurotransmitter.

Regardless, after the binding process, the receiving neuron undergoes various changes, as well. Chemical reactions are triggered, and inside the neuron, the neurotransmitter's message is transported in either its original form or a modified form depending on the specific neurotransmitter and receptor. This message passes into the axon, and from there, to the next neuron or set of neurons. Eventually, the original message, or a version that has undergone modifications, reaches a final destination, affecting what and how we behave, feel, and think.

So let's take the sample case of Amity and examine briefly the possible neuroscience explanation of why they think and behave as they do. Members of the Amity faction are peaceful and happy, high on life, it seems. Most likely, their brains contain a lot of the neurotransmitter called dopamine. It's possible to have a lot of dopamine in your brain due to genetic reasons. But it's also possible to have a lot of dopamine in the brain due to the ingestion of pills, or in the case of Amity, simply the foods they eat. The Amity are responsible for growing food and delivering it to the city. We know, for example, that Johanna tells Four and Tris to avoid eating Amity's bread, which contains a peace serum.

It's possible that the peace serum contains the same type of chemicals in the pleasurable and addictive aspects of drugs. The odd thing is that nobody in Amity seems to have died from too much of a good thing, be it dopamine or some other trigger that counteracts negative, moody thoughts. In the real world, we know that many teens can't take the same antidepressants as adults, that these same medicines can cause teen suicides. So I wonder how the children and teenagers in the world of *Divergent* handle the same peace serums as the adults. Also of interest is the fact that the peace serum wears off after five hours, which is not the case with real-life antidepressants. But for now, let's return to the idea that perhaps the Amity have a lot of dopamine coursing through their brains.

Dopamine is the most prominent type of neuroactive substance associated with what happens when you take drugs and get high, feel great pleasure, and also get addicted. (Neuroactive substances include both neurotransmitters and neuromodulators, but for the sake of simplicity in this book, I refer to all neuroactive substances simply as neurotransmitters.) Dopamine is associated with the reward and pleasure centers in the brain. It affects the processes in the brain that control such things as experiencing pleasure and pain, responding emotionally to happy and sad events, and being motivated to do things, and it also affects processes that control our movements. In the latter case, we know that the neurons containing dopamine reside in the substantia nigra section of the basal ganglia in the midbrain. You might remember that the basal ganglia are responsible for our movements, so people with Parkinson's disease and ALS have problems with the number of dopamine-containing neurons in their basal ganglia. Drugs such as L-DOPA for Parkinson's disease are converted in the brain to dopamine.

Both cocaine and amphetamines, which make people feel euphoric, increase the amount of dopamine in the synaptic clefts of neurons. They stimulate the brain and interfere with the reuptake of dopamine, and amphetamines also contribute to the release of more dopamine at the nerve terminals.

Dopamine itself is classified as a monoamine, and if you want to get more specific, it's in the monoamine subcategory of catecholamine. Along with dopamine is norepinephrine, which regulates such things as moods and dreaming. Both dopamine and norepinephrine, along with another neurotransmitter called epinephrine, are synthesized from the amino acid tyrosine in a common manner using the same five enzymes. If we want to seek a genetic factor in the Amity's regard for euphoria and happiness, peace and love, we could look to the fact that three of these five enzymes seem to be linked together on the same chromosome.

The other subcategory of monoamine is called an indoleamine and includes serotonin. All four of the monamine neurotransmitters are released at the synaptic junctures between neurons. And all four relate to mood and mental states.

The Amity most likely have a lot of serotonin reuptake inhibitors in their brains, as well. Both serotonin and norepinephrine reuptake inhibitors, commonly referred to as SNRIs, are modern drugs that help people who are battling depression. Sometimes they're also used to treat serious pain in the nervous system. SNRIs block the reuptake, or absorption, of serotonin and norepinephrine, which in turn, helps neurons send and receive messages and helps you feel happier. One reason a drug like LSD makes a person high is that it affects serotonin receptors.

Then there are endorphins, which neurons release when we're stressed or in pain. They increase states of relaxation, calm, and dreaminess. Drugs such as morphine and heroin increase the release of endorphins. It's possible the Amity also have more than a usual amount of endorphins in their brains, too.

In addition to chemicals, we can look at the two major hemispheres of the brain in an attempt to analyze the basic neuroscience of, say, the Amity. The left hemisphere of the brain probably is responsible for achievement in rational, intellectual, and analytical matters, so we might think of the Erudite as having more neurotransmissions and synapses in their left hemispheres than in their right; conversely, the Amity might have reduced activity in their left hemispheres and enhanced activity in the right. It's the right hemisphere that is said to excel in emotional and intuitive thinking, and sensory experiences. Please note that I'm simplifying the description of the hemispheres because this is a companion guide about *Divergent* rather than a text about the brain! My underlying point is that each faction can be explained by brain chemistry and possibly by genetics, as well.

Our genes encode proteins that directly affect the development and regulation of our neural circuits, which in turn, affect our behavior. Over the years, the environment in which we live also affects our neural circuitry and, hence, our behavior.

Experts tell us that there are two forms of behavior, instinctive and learned. Instinctive behaviors depend quite a bit on our genetic makeup, while learned behaviors are obviously picked up over time. Instinctive behaviors include sex and emotions, and while it can be controversial to claim that our behaviors are inherited, in some ways, this might be the case. For example, experts believe that schizophrenia and bipolar affective disorder are both dependent upon genetic makeup. It could be that multiple genes are involved, but evidence also suggests that environmental factors are important, too. What we do know is that behavior develops over time and, at first, largely depends on genetic factors. Also, we know that environmental factors begin to affect behavior even in utero, while a person is still a fetus.

So is it possible to manipulate genes to change a person as described in *Allegiant*? Remember, the Bureau of Genetic Welfare traced violence to a so-called murder gene and also found a lot of additional genes that contributed to "bad" personality traits. If society is "broken," as the Bureau believed, can we actually manipulate genes to create a new society? Sadly, the answer is yes; it may be possible in the not-so-distant future to manipulate genes and overhaul personalities as well as intelligence, appearance, and other factors.

Different genes are activated in different cells and for

different reasons. Some genes, which are active in many cells, help the cells make proteins. Other genes are relatively inactive—for example, those that are related to the development of a fetus. After this type of gene completes its function, it shuts down. Still other genes are specific to a cell type, such as a brain cell. In general, a cell activates the genes it needs for whatever function it's performing at a certain time, and it suppresses all the genes that are unrelated to the function.

These basic attributes of genes and cells are key to understanding how scientists such as those in *Allegiant* manipulate genes in an attempt to eliminate violent and supposed "bad" traits from human begins. Indeed, it may also be possible to change the genetic makeup of an unborn child. If, for example, the Allegiant scientists know how to alter a brain cell's genetic constitution to remove mental illness, then they can either fix the genes of mentally ill people or make sure the children of the mentally ill have the traits desired by the scientists.

Very creepy scenarios, of course, but they're also very real. A lot of it is happening already.

Our genes determine how our bodies fight illnesses and infections, combat poisons, and digest foods. Our genes determine our appearances and, in many cases, how we behave and how we react to emotional stimuli.

In addition, our bodies have mutated genes inherited from one or both of our parents, and these mutated genes may cause thousands of different diseases. An inherited mutation is in almost every cell of the body. When the cells divide, the mutation is reproduced in the new cells. This inherited type of mutation is called a germline mutation, because it involves the egg and sperm, or the germ cells.

If scientists create the germline mutations, as they do in *Allegiant*, then they are altering a person's basic attributes. In the real world, this is known as germline manipulation. Specifically, what might happen—again, in our real world, not *just* in the fictional world of *Divergent*—is that scientists modify the genes in a fertilized egg, which is the first cell in an embryo. These genetic changes are then reproduced in all subsequent cells of the embryo . . . and ultimately, in the baby. Note that the genetic changes are also copied into the reproductive cells, meaning that the changes will continue throughout the generations.

But genetic modifications go far beyond changing the genes in the reproductive cells. Scientists in the real world can also change existing body cells of a grown person. These cells are called somatic cells. When genetic modifications occur in somatic cells, do future generations also have the genetic changes? No, they don't. In real life, doctors might change the genes of somatic cells in order to treat illnesses such as cystic fibrosis.

Germline experimentation and research using people can be quite dangerous and for obvious reasons. Would you want a scientist messing with your genes, your personality, the essence of who you are . . . and by extension, with your children's genes, personality, and basic humanity? Probably not.

Scientists routinely conduct germline research using other animals, such as mice. Within the next decade or so, human germline research may be common, as well. Again, this is scary, but true; and what Veronica Roth describes in *Allegiant* is really quite conceivable. If the wrong people get their hands on this type of technology, and if these people happen to be in power, well, anything's possible, right?

In 2001, the BBC reported a successful experiment of germline engineering, in which thirty genetically altered babies were born healthy, half of them from an "experimental programme at a U.S. laboratory."[1] When doctors genetically tested the babies, they found that they did indeed contain genes not inherited from their parents. Scientists added genes to the babies, who someday, will supply these new genes to their children.

The scientists in *Allegiant* use genetic trackers to determine if a person's genes have actually changed. They also do genetic scans to determine the genetic composition a person has and what might be missing. As with genetic manipulation, these techniques aren't particularly far-fetched.

In the real world, doctors use genetic testing to determine if conditions are ripe for a person to develop particular diseases and illnesses. You can think of these genetic tests as the "genetic scans" in *Allegiant*. Doctors perform genetic tests to determine if a baby or a fetus has genetic disorders. They perform genetic tests to find out if a person carries a mutated gene that causes a disease. They also test to determine if a person who has been diagnosed with a disease actually has that disease. In fact, we have many hundreds of genetic tests already in clinical use.

As of 2013, the United States Food and Drug Administration identified approved genetic tests for diseases such as:[2]

- Acute myeloid leukemia
- B-cell chronic lymphocytic leukemia
- Bladder cancer
- Breast cancer
- Cystic fibrosis
- Chromosome abnormalities

The National Institutes of Health maintain a Genetic Testing Registry that lists and describes a wide variety of genetic tests. On their Web site, they've cataloged more than 45,000 sequence variations and how those variations affect our health. They also indicate that laboratories have already registered "over 12,000 [genetic] tests for 3,500 conditions!"[3] In addition, according to the National Human Genome Research Institute in 2005, "We may be able to have our genomes sequenced for $1,000 in 10 years' time."[4]

If we legally are allowed to predict our children's propensities for diseases and other traits (such as violence in *Allegiant*), then what happens to us as a society? If we can test fetuses for hundreds of genetic diseases, then the possibility exists that people will use this information to prevent the birth of "damaged" babies. Perhaps the fetuses will be aborted. Or perhaps, as in *Allegiant,* doctors will change the genes in our reproductive cells and simply avoid the birth of "damaged" babies.

On the flip side, genetic modifications could actually save lives. Perhaps we can avoid the suffering and deaths related to brain tumors, various forms of cancer, anemia, cystic fibrosis, and high cholesterol that possibly leads to heart attacks and strokes.

But who draws the lines about what's valid? Who decides if a baby, for example, should undergo genetic modifications to be treated for possible high cholesterol or brain tumors as opposed to a predisposition for violence and crime?

In our real world, the ethical and even social ramifications of genetic testing remain a battlefield. If we're all tested for possible genetic damage, or GD in *Allegiant* terminology, then we'll carry the stigma of whatever supposed genetic damages we possess. This means that employers may not hire us, or they may fire us when they learn of our genetic damages. It means that friends and even family may view us differently. Remember Tobias's reaction to learning that he is genetically damaged? He totally flips out, feels inferior and embarrassed, somehow deficient as a human being.

Lori Andrews, an internationally recognized expert on the legal issues involved with genetics and biotechnologies, writes that in "an extraordinary breach of privacy, one company even put identifiable patients' medical records on the Internet without their consent, which allowed tissue buyers to learn more about the patients who were the sources of the cell lines." She fears the time when schools, courts, and health insurance providers demand that we all obtain and report genetic tests. She fears the time when these social institutions test us without our consent or knowledge. In fact, she writes, it may also be true that already, "insurers, employers, or courts may be making decisions about us based on our genes."[5]

"To what extent," asks Mark Rothstein, professor of law and director of the Health Law and Policy Institute at the University of Houston, "will the accumulation of genetic information increase the stigma on individuals who are currently affected or who may be affected in the future (their family members and others)? What is the prospect for eugenics?" As noted above, genetic testing and manipulations do indeed increase the chance that people will abort "damaged" babies, but it also raises the possibility of *murder*: the killing of people with "damaged" genes.[6]

Futurist Michael Zey predicts that by 2020, we'll routinely perform genetic modifications to correct diseases as well as "an individual's vulnerability to developing a specific disease."[7]

In the world of *Allegiant,* when the scientists toy with people's genes, they accidentally mess everything up. The genetic modifications don't work as they plan. Well, it makes sense, doesn't it? If we can manipulate genes to eliminate diseases or problems, then we can manipulate genes to *cause* diseases or problems, too. In fact, genetic modifications may become a method of both suicide and homicide in the future. If we can figure out how to overcome cancer via genetic modifications, then we might also figure out how to *cause* cancer using the same techniques. Or schizophrenia, hand tremors, blindness, and so on and so on . . .

As happens in *Allegiant,* in the process of learning how to eliminate diseases and "bad" personality traits, scientists could accidentally cause unforeseen problems. This is a real danger. Say we modify several genes to cure a form of cancer, but by manipulating these genes, we also trigger another problem in the person's body? What if a gene has multiple functions? Perhaps it contributes to a form of cancer, but when suppressed, it contributes to a form of blindness? In a real-world example, when researchers inserted foreign DNA into mouse embryos, the mice were born with serious defects. They didn't have any eyes. Portions of their inner ears were missing. And they also couldn't smell correctly.[8]

Years ago, I downloaded a free poster from the Human Genome Project, which identifies all known diseases linked to specific chromosomes. You can stop by the Web site[9] today and download your own copy should you be interested in the potentials of genetic manipulations in the real world. We can safely assume that the scientists in *Allegiant* know all about these diseases linked to specific chromosomes. Who knows what they've been curing, fixing, and . . . mangling? Here are some examples: Chromosome #1 has 263 million bases and genetic links that cause dozens and possibly hundreds of problems, including glycogen storage disease, acute leukemia, colon cancer, cataracts, glaucoma, migraines, and susceptibility to measles. Chromosome #2 has 255 million bases and genetic links that cause dozens and possibly hundreds of problems, too, including ovarian cancer, cleft palate, cataracts, obesity, and epilepsy. You may have noticed that both Chromosomes #1 and #2 have genes that affect a person's susceptibility to cataracts. If scientists "fix" Chromosome #1 to eliminate cataracts, must they also "fix" Chromosome #2? And if they do fix both, is it possible that they'll accidentally trigger something dreadful in the person such as cerebral palsy?

As germline engineering becomes more prevalent (and legal), parents will use it to make sure their babies are born in good health. They'll screen embryos and want to correct genetic defects with germline therapy. As the techniques improve and become safer and more accepted, this is when we have to worry about things such as the genetic manipulations in *Allegiant*. At first, germline engineering will probably be used with in vitro fertilization, whereby the doctor will remove a mother's egg and fertilize it, then grow the fertilized egg into an embryo. He will then perform some type of genetic manipulation and put the embryo back into the mother.

If we manipulate genes so almost everyone has supposed "perfect" or "desirable" traits—GP, or genetic purity, to use the *Allegiant* terminology—then what are we doing to the human race? The *Allegiant* scientists basically want to eliminate the *diversity* that makes each of us special and unique, the *diversity* that enables the human race to survive. By modifying the genetics of an entire population, the *Allegiant* scientists put the human race at great risk.

A final topic related to neuroscience and genetics relates to the Divergents and their mirror neurons. In the real world, scientists claim that people who exhibit empathy toward others have *more mirror neurons,* which operate like natural predictors of other people's intentions. Well, we know that the Abnegation are highly emphatic toward others: they're the ones responsible for charity and they exhibit great selflessness. This may be why more Divergent, with their "flexible" minds and abundance of mirror neurons, come from the Abnegation faction than any other known faction. But let's move to the next chapter and find out what all of this means.

4

THE DIVERGENT AND MIRROR NEURONS

The Divergent seem to blend all that's best about each other faction. They possess the selflessness of Abnegation, the honesty of Candor, the intelligence of Erudite, the bravery of Dauntless, and the desire for peace of the Amity. However, they possess these traits in moderation. This means they don't give up everything and forsake their own needs, as the Abnegation do. They don't prize Erudite intelligence and knowledge so much that they coldly analyze everything without regard for the humane. They don't always tell the Candor truth, babbling constantly without making decisions. They don't turn into Dauntless bullies, and while they desire Amity peace, they're smart enough to realize that quite often, peace comes at great cost.

Jeanine and her scientists explain that the Divergent mind has an abundance of mirror neurons, which, as is true in reality, enable someone to empathize with others and understand what others intend to do based on their behaviors. According to Jeanine, having a lot of mirror neurons leads a Divergent person such as Tris to be flexible in the way she thinks and results in her tests displaying aptitude for multiple factions. In reality, we all display different levels of empathy and aptitudes. In reality, genetics, brain chemistry, and our environment affect the way we think—in other words, our aptitudes and abilities to empathize are based on much more than how many mirror neurons we have in our brains.

In addition, Jeanine's MRI of Tris's brain shows that Tris has an unusually large lateral prefrontal cortex and a small orbitofrontal cortex. Supposedly, Tris does well in making decisions and achieving goals due to her large lateral prefrontal cortex, and she doesn't care much about getting rewards for her behavior due to her small orbitofrontal cortex. Is it true, as Tris worries, that the size of our brain sections determines who we are and what we do, that our brain anatomy defines our entire personalities?

Let's first address the question about mirror neurons. Why does a person with a substantial number of mirror neurons display increased empathy toward others? Does this factor increase our aptitude for such things as bravery, raw intelligence, loving peace, always telling the truth, and selfless behavior?

At the University of Parma in Italy, researchers studying motor-command neurons in monkeys noticed that sometimes the neurons fired when a monkey saw another monkey do something. In other words, one monkey's neurons *mirrored* the firing of another monkey's neurons. In the early 1990s, neuroscientist Giacomo Rizzolatti, along with Giuseppe di Pellegrino, Luciano Fadiga, Leonardo Fogassi, and Vittorio Gallese, placed electrodes in the brains of macaque monkeys in a section called the ventral premotor cortex. Their objective was to study the motor neurons responsible for controlling the actions of a monkey's hands and mouth. They wanted to know what happened in the brain when the monkey picked up food, and as the monkey reached for and lifted food in their experiments, the scientists recorded what single neurons were doing. They were amazed that the monkey's neurons fired when one of the men picked up a banana. In other words, the monkey hadn't picked it up. Rather, it had seen the man do it.

In loose terms, the monkey experienced similar sensations in both doing and observing the same actions. It could put itself in the place of the man and perceive his actions as if the monkey were performing them. Because primates are social animals, it's possible that their brains evolved to include these neurons that enable primates to imitate others and also anticipate what others are going to do.

In 1996, the scientists published a paper, in which they reported that they "recorded electrical activity from 532 neurons" in two monkeys and discovered properties of what they called mirror neurons. These neurons "became active both when the monkey performed a given action and when it observed a similar action performed by the experimenter." Further, they posited that "a matching system, similar to that of mirror neurons, exists in humans and could be involved in recognition of actions as well as phonetic gestures."[1]

Then in 2004, Rizzolatti and Laila Craighero of the University of Ferrara, published a paper called "The Mirror-Neuron System." In this paper, they explained that if humans "want to survive, we must understand the actions of others." In addition, if we can't understand others, we cannot function in a "social organization," which I assume means society. The bit of amazing information in this paper was that the scientists described the properties in the human mirror-neuron system that might "explain the human capacity to learn by imitation."[2]

Then in 2010, scientists analyzed 139 imaging studies of the human brain and confirmed that we have mirror neurons in the same parts of our brains where monkeys have them. In addition, in 2010 researchers placed electrodes in the brains of twenty-one patients suffering from epilepsy and were able to record actual mirror-neuron activities. This was the first time scientists had recorded the activities of mirror neurons in human brains.[3]

Especially interesting is that, in 2010, the scientists also detected mirror neurons in the medial temporal lobe of the human brain. It's possible that this explains why people sometimes *think* they've performed actions that somebody else actually performed. But this is just a theory.

A key expert in all of this is Giacomo Rizzolatti, who led the original research. As recently as 2011, he reported that people recognize emotions in others thanks to their mirror neurons.

In humans, mirror neurons are more like *mirror-neuron systems,* as reflected by the title of Rizzolatti and Craighero's 2004 paper. They are sophisticated enough to interpret the complicated intentions of others and imitate complex actions.

As such, it's possible that mirror neurons helped shape the evolution of language in humans. Consider that they may enable us to mimic sounds—that is, tongue and mouth movements.

For example, the left inferior parietal lobe of the monkey brain is rich in mirror neurons, and we also know that it is crucial in human language.

Mirror neurons are also found in the anterior cingulate cortex, which is a key interface between emotions and cognitions, converting our feelings into actions and intended actions. In addition, the anterior cingulate cortex enables us to adapt to changing conditions and control our emotions. And it's also where sensory pain neurons respond to the pain receptors in the skin.

Suppose two patients are in the same room. A doctor enters and does something that causes pain in one of the patients. Perhaps he sticks a needle in a knee joint or in the spinal cord. The other patient might very well flinch. His sensory pain neurons might very well respond as if the needle were sliding into him instead of the other patient.

In 1999, Senior Scientist William D. Hutchison of the University of Toronto and his associates indeed witnessed this type of reaction.[4] Tania Singer and Boris C. Bernhardt of the Max Planck Institute for Human Cognitive and Brain Sciences in Germany co-published a paper in July of 2012, which stated that "Empathy—the ability to share the feelings of others—is fundamental to our emotional and social lives" and that previous research consistently showed "activations in regions also involved in the direct pain experience." The paper points to the anterior insula and anterior and midcingulate cortex.[5]

If you're wondering if the mirror neurons in Tris's brain enable her to experience the pain of others, to empathize with them, then this is your answer. The research does indeed suggest that mirror neurons play a part in blurring the boundary between ourselves and others.

So if this is the case, then why don't people such as Tris

and Four—and basically all the Divergent—feel everybody's pain all the time? And why don't they imitate every action around them? What keeps the mirror neurons in check?

You have to keep in mind that scientists are still examining how our brains work, and answers to all our questions are as yet unknown. So possibly, our brains include inhibitory neural circuits that circumvent automatic imitations of inappropriate actions. The left inferior parietal lobe continually supplies us with a variety of possible actions we can take, but our frontal cortex accepts only one of each set and rejects all the others. Harking back to free will, it may be that this neural mechanism of suppression of all but one action in a particular scenario is how we make our own choices.

As for why the Divergent don't constantly feel everybody else's pain, this is a tough question to answer. Perhaps the frontal cortex and its inhibitory circuits save us from this terrible fate. Or perhaps they work in conjunction with the fact that *our* skin doesn't actually feel the pain of the needle. Somehow, the brain knows that when the mirror neurons fire and when the sensory pain neurons go wild, we haven't been injected, we're only witnessing somebody else's pain.

Another question I've been pondering is this: With the exception of Abnegation, why are mirror neurons so incredibly lacking in the brains of people in the other factions? Is it logical that a Dauntless, for example, can imitate complicated movements required to leap off speeding trains and tall buildings without getting killed yet not be able to use his mirror neurons for empathy? If a Dauntless has sufficient mirror neurons to help him imitate the highly skilled maneuvers of an expert knife thrower, then why can't he also express empathy?

Clearly, it could be that other parts of the brain are engaged when the Dauntless learn to mimic complex actions.

Perhaps the empathy and mimicry require a lot more than a dense thicket of mirror neurons. If this is the case, then the fact that the Divergent brains contain more mirror neurons really wouldn't matter as much as we might think.

Again, this is all speculation. We're talking about ongoing research.

We discussed the Divergent a bit in the last chapter in regard to the Aptitude Tests. Remember, Tris is thought to be Divergent and must hide this fact at all costs because she conquers the simulations with ease. Her brain is flexible enough to do this, we are told. Much later, we learn about Tris's mirror neurons when Jeanine does the brain scan on her. I'm not sure that I can figure out the connection between mirror neurons and the "flexible" brain that conquers simulations and hence displays "equal aptitude" for Dauntless, Erudite, and Abnegation. Other attributes of the brain far beyond mirror neurons must be key to both Dauntless and Erudite traits. Otherwise, Dauntless and Erudite would be equally represented along with Abnegation within the Divergent population. It seems that a person who displays traits of Abnegation, Dauntless, and Erudite is not necessarily Divergent, with its abundance of mirror neurons.

I also wonder how the Divergent brain is wired—well beyond mirror neurons—to be capable of resisting powerful serums packed with transmitters. It's true that different people's brains react to the same drugs in different ways. But it's quite another thing to suggest that some people's brains are wired so they completely reject drugs, serums, and in this futuristic scenario, serums with computer transmitters. In *Allegiant,* we're told that it all has to do with restoring "genetically damaged" people to a "genetically pure" state. A person whose genes have been "healed" is Divergent. It all makes for a great story, and in fact, everything about the neuroscience and psychology in these books combines to supply us with a terrific set of novels. But I was still puzzling over the Divergent capabilities at the end of *Allegiant*.

Tris's mother defines Divergent brains as moving "in a dozen different directions." She tells Tris that the Divergent cannot be controlled, because they are not "confined to one way of thinking." At this point, toward the end of the *Divergent* novel, I started thinking that the Factionless might all be Divergent, possibly of a weaker form than Tris and Four. I'll delve more into the Factionless in the next chapter, but for now, it's interesting to note that they come from all the other factions; they don't fit into their original factions or their chosen factions. They can't make it through initiation, so possibly, their Divergent minds aren't as strong as Tris's and Four's minds. This idea is supported by Jeanine's comment that Tris has one of the strongest Divergent minds. Again, this is speculation on my part.

Shifting for a moment to the notion that the Divergent mind is "flexible," we might instead use the term "creative," which derives from the Latin *creare*. A creative mind tends to piece together information from a variety of sources to reach new conclusions, to produce or think of something that does not currently exist. Originality might be defined as the perception of novel relationships and often includes the ability to devise ways of implementing what is perceived. Some creative minds lean toward theory, while others can take the theories and create something from them. A creative mind tends to hear, visualize, and think of things *differently*.

Creative individuals often have some combination of these personality traits:

- Adventurous
- Rebellious
- Persistent
- Curious
- Sensitive
- Open to new experiences and ideas
- Individuality.

This could be a description of both Tris and Four. In fact, it provides a very good portrayal of the Divergent people, who are open to new experiences and ideas, and who are not afraid to pursue them. In very broad terms: as in reality, the Divergent do not wear the blinders of conventionalism, meaning they observe things differently and have a built-in tolerance for other viewpoints and ways of doing things.

In addition (and again, in very broad terms), the creative person—or Divergent—tends to shun imposed social rules that make little sense to him. Instead, he follows internally generated rules that do make sense to him. While not particularly interested in conventional rules, this type of person also displays sensitivity or empathy toward others. The creative/Divergent mind is able to see things from other viewpoints and also observe things from his own viewpoint in richer detail and clarity.

Persistence is also critical to the creative/Divergent, because when you think and act outside of normal, conventional boundaries, you tend to be rejected, isolated, and often misunderstood even by those closest to you. Such a person must persist to be herself and follow her own directions and ideas.

You can see that, although I'm speaking in very general terms, all these traits that psychologists assign to creative individuals also apply to the Divergent.

In fact, psychologists who devise creativity tests and study creative people have a word for the ability to come up with many different paths and options. They have a word to define the personality traits I listed above. Take one guess: What's this one word?

Divergent.

The word for conventional thinking, by the way, is *convergent,* describing a person who finds one right answer to a problem. Each faction seems to fall under this definition of convergent, for each thinks it has come up with the one solution to society's problems.

It's not simply a matter of higher intelligence, as the Erudite think. Creativity—that is, Divergent thinking—is different from simple IQ.

French psychologist Alfred Binet is credited with devising the first intelligence quotient test. In simple terms, Binet measured intelligence with this formula:

$$IQ = (MA/CA) \times 100$$

where CA is a person's chronological or actual age in years and MA is the person's mental age based on test performance. For example, if a child is ten years old and his mental age is measured as being the same as a twelve-year-old, then the child's IQ is 120.

The original tests covered a person's knowledge of facts and how this type of knowledge increased with age. Some children, for example, knew more than others at the age of two or twelve.

In 1916 at Stanford University, Lewis Terman revised Binet's tests and published the Stanford–Binet Intelligence Scale test for use in the United States. In 1921, Terman began a study that would make him famous. He was interested in children who were approximately ten and eleven years old and with IQ measurements of 135 to 200, averaging somewhere in the range of 150. Terman studied these "genius-level" individuals for seventy years. What made his study interesting was that he measured intelligence far beyond the ability to remember facts. He also measured his subjects' marriages, emotional development, physical attributes, social circumstances, occupational achievements, and health. But what's also interesting when thinking about creative people and the Divergent is that very few of the "genius-level" individuals in Terman's study actually created anything truly new and amazing in their lifetimes. Of course, some of the people were brilliant and did well in art, music, literature, science, and so forth, but generally, while Terman's subjects achieved material and societal success, they didn't exhibit much in the way of striking creativity.

Scientists don't really know what makes a mind Divergent, or highly creative. Many studies have been done, and many theories are out there.

This brings me to Jeanine's MRI of Tris's brain, which we're told shows that Tris has an unusually large lateral prefrontal cortex and a small orbitofrontal cortex. We're further told that the large lateral prefrontal cortex helps her with decisions and goals. The small orbitofrontal cortex means she doesn't care much about being rewarded for what she does.

The brain has three main parts, forebrain, midbrain, and hindbrain. In the forebrain is the cerebrum or cortex, thalamus, and hypothalamus, which are all part of the limbic system. The cortex is the largest section of the human brain, and it has four parts called lobes: frontal lobe, parietal lobe, occipital lobe, and temporal lobe.

The frontal lobe of the cortex handles planning, movement, problem solving, and reasoning. In short, it enables us to make decisions and plan goals for ourselves. Both Tris's brain areas mentioned by Jeanine are in the frontal cortex. The lateral prefrontal cortex helps determine and is critically involved in the control and planning of our actions and behaviors.

The orbitofrontal cortex helps us make decisions, as well, and also represents the area involved in making decisions based on perceived rewards.

But to paraphrase an old saying in a different context, *Does size really matter?*

Well, it was reported in 2010 that people who are introspective and able to reflect upon their decisions have "larger" anterior prefrontal cortexes.[6] However, it could be that it's the number, variety, density, and strength of neuronal interconnections that make the difference. After all, the cortex has folds that increase the surface area and enable more interconnections, so sheer "size" may not be the key. If neurons are tightly packed, they transmit information to one another more quickly and efficiently.

In addition, it might make sense to take into account the size of a person's overall body in relation to brain size. In other words, if you're six feet ten inches tall and weigh four hundred pounds, your brain size might be proportionate to your body. This same brain in the body of a four-feet-two-inch-tall woman weighing seventy pounds might be considered huge.

The correlation of larger brain size to more intelligence, in general, has long been debated by experts. Many people point to Albert Einstein, whose brain was on the "smaller" end of "average" human size,[7] though it must be noted that certain parts of his brain—such as the inferior parietal region, which is connected to our mathematical abilities—were larger than most.

But also, as reported by *The Telegraph*, Einstein's brain had an "unusually high number of folds and grooves," and according to Florida State University anthropologist Dean Falk, "regions that are exceptionally complicated in their convolutions."[8]

Yet this same article in *The Telegraph* also notes that Einstein's prefrontal cortex, "linked to concentration and forward planning," was larger than most.[9] In addition, as Professor Michael E. Martinez, author of *Future Bright* from Oxford University Press writes in *Salon*, we know that the prefrontal cortex is indeed "the single brain area consistently activated by a broad array of intelligence tests."[10]

In the end, even if we're talking about the most "Divergent" person of all, Albert Einstein, experts still don't know what made his brain so special. To quote Professor Martinez, "The correlation between intelligence and brain size is far from perfect, as Einstein's brain vividly illustrates. Clearly, the relationship between brain size and IQ falls short of a complete account of how the brain relates to intelligence."[11]

So is it true, as Tris worries, that the size of our brain sections determines who we are and what we do, that our brain anatomy defines our entire personalities? Probably literal size does not matter. More likely, the neural connections and densities, and the plasticity of our minds—that is, how the connections grow and interconnect over time—are also vital. Her questions are interesting, and it's worth repeating that even scientists at the forefront of brain research in the real world don't have all the answers.

As for her orbitofrontal cortex size leading to her lack of concern about being rewarded for the good deeds she does, other parts of the brain are also part of the "reward pathway." Sometimes this pathway is called the mesolimbic dopamine system, or MDS, and at other times, it's called the medial forebrain bundle. Perhaps these other areas are also augmented and are denser with neurons, synapses, and interconnections than in most people's brains.

Looking at the brain from the center to the front, the following areas are the main ones involved in the MDS reward pathway: the ventral tegmental area, which resides near the amygdala toward the lower center of the brain; the nucleus accumbens, found approximately halfway between the center to the front of the brain; and the frontal and prefrontal cortex. Because most of the current neuroscience research that uses brain imaging focuses on the frontal lobes, this may be why Jeanine looks at brain images of Tris's orbitofrontal cortex. And yet, *Divergent* must be rather far into our future, given the sophisticated serum technology, so we would expect Jeanine to look at the other sections in the reward pathway, as well.

Mirror neurons are triggered, as psychotherapist F. Diane Barth writes, "when someone else is sad, angry, or unhappy, and . . . those mirror neurons help us feel what that other person is feeling . . . what they actually help us feel is what we would experience if we were in that person's place."[12] In short, the Divergent may indeed possess considerable *empathy*, which is in short supply in the real world and which is desperately needed in Tris's world.

FACTIONS AND THE FACTIONLESS

AUTHORITARIAN RULE AND PREJUDICES

When asked where she got the idea for the Divergent series, Veronica Roth says she started wondering how our moral codes can change, given the right conditions, after she learned about the Milgram experiment. In the bonus materials in the back of the *Divergent* novel, she briefly notes that the experiment shed light on how we view authority figures and why we obey them.

By understanding the power of authority, we might be able to determine why the people in all the factions obey their leaders regardless of the cost, including casting their own family members into a homeless and supposedly miserable and lonely

existence as the Factionless. This is true even of Abnegation. While members of Abnegation provide food and aid
for the Factionless, they are also quite capable of letting
their own children end up Factionless should they fail their
initiations.

In addition, by understanding how such extreme prejudice can occur, we might get a grasp on why the people in all
the factions, except perhaps Abnegation, are capable of ignor-
ing the Factionless.

But first, let's address the Milgram experiment. In the field
of social psychology, early researchers began delving into authority issues after they escaped from Nazi Germany and made
their way to the United States.

Theodor W. Adorno with his colleagues, for example, came
up with idea of an authoritarian personality. Adorno left Germany in 1934, and while the Nazis were in power, he lived in
Oxford, New York City, and also California. He wrote *The Authoritarian Personality* during that period, although the 990-
page book was published later in 1950 by Harper & Brothers.[1]
Adorno returned to Germany in 1949.

In the 1950 book, he devised methods for defining the
personality traits that lead to fascist behavior in an individual.
In addition, he ranked the traits on what he defined as the
F-scale. The argument was loosely that if an individual's experiences as a child lead to nine specific personality traits,
then that child may very well grow up to be a fascist. If the
child's parents are exceedingly strict and punish him a lot,
then in time, the child will possess a huge amount of anger
toward his parents. But he'll be too afraid of them to express
his anger toward them. Instead, he'll begin to idolize other
authority figures and will express his anger outward: toward
other people.

Here are some of the traits identified as leading a person toward a highly prejudiced state of mind and a right-wing authoritarian outlook:

1. Blind allegiance to black-and-white conventional definitions of right and wrong.

2. Belief that violence is justified against people who don't agree with conventional definitions of right and wrong, who are different from the individual in question, and who don't submit to conventional authority figures. Seeking such people, condemning and punishing them.

3. Strong resistance to new ideas, creativity, and subjective thinking. Anything less than the tough-minded conventional method is dangerous to "our" society and "our" way of thinking. Belief in simple polemics and answers with no room for other opinions and viewpoints. An example might be the belief that all "our" problems are caused by loose morals in society.

4. Rigid categorization of everything, including people. Stereotyping. Superstition. Belief that supernatural or mystic things determine our fates.

5. Obsession with dominant–submissive ways of viewing the world: strong versus weak. Strong adherence to leaders who use uncompromising power to obtain their objectives. Identifying with authority figures. Unrealistic and exaggerated view of personal toughness and strength.

6. Built-in scapegoating of other groups of people based on internal and typically subconscious feelings of inadequacy and rage. The world is a wild and dangerous place.

7. Obsession with sex.

"It was clear," wrote the authors of *The Authoritarian Personality* on page 223, that "anti-Semitism and ethnocentrism were not merely matters of surface opinion, but general tendencies with sources, in part at least, deep within the structure of the person." And their study and the F-scale went far beyond anti-Semitism and ethnocentrism and attempted to provide a much more "comprehensive grasp of the prejudiced outlook on the world." (page 224)

In the F-scale are questions that remind me a great deal of the various factions in *Divergent*. For example, one question requires people to define how much they agree with certain statements, such as:

Some people are born with the urge to jump from high places.

No weakness or difficulty can hold us back if we have enough willpower.

Doesn't this remind you of the way the *Dauntless* think?

WHERE DO YOU RANK ON THE AUTHORITARIAN F-SCALE?

There are far too many questions on the real F-scale to pose here, but to give you a better idea of how it works, you can try answering these samples from the real F-scale test and judging for yourself where you might fit on the scale of prejudice and rigid opinion.[2]

If you answer in ways that mean you might believe in strict authoritarian rule, then you might be the type of person who ends up following leaders such as Jeanine Matthews and Eric.

If you want to truly test yourself, then you probably have to see a psychiatrist and ask him to use Form 78 of Adorno's F-scale measurements.

How much do you agree with the following statements? Read each statement; then jot down or just think about the level to which you agree with it. In each case, I'll supply my own analysis of the results. That is, if you strongly agree with a statement, I'll give you *my opinion* as to whether the agreement correlates to the various personality traits on Adorno's F-scale.

The important thing is for *you* to assess yourself. Even if you read the 990-page *The Authoritarian Personality,* you'll see that assessing yourself on the F-scale is indeed difficult, and that's putting it mildly. Certain statements suggest a direct correlation to specific traits, yet depending on how strongly you agree with the statements, multiple traits could be at play. As pointed out on page 240, when briefly reviewing the trait Obsession with Sex, "concern with overt sexuality is represented in the F-scale by four items, two of which have appeared in connection with authoritarian aggression and one other as an expression of projectivity." In short, the authors of the book also point out that the variables are significant in number and they closely overlap and interact with each other.

As an aside, I find it very amusing that on page 243, the authors of the book state that there "appears to be no ready explanation for the low reliability found in the case of the Public Speaking Men." Perhaps this is a general comment about our difficulty in finding government leaders who say what they really mean, remain consistent in what they say, and have our best interests at heart. Or perhaps this is a general comment related to the possibility that some of our leaders have fascist tendencies while others do not.

This is certainly true in the *Divergent* series, in which some leaders—such as Tris's father—are genuine people who say what they really mean, remain consistent in what they say, and have our best interests at heart. Other leaders in Tris's world are the opposite, such as Jeanine and Eric.

But let's move on to the F-scale test!

1. **America is getting so far from the true American way of life that force may be necessary to restore it.**

If you strongly agree with this statement, then you probably possess the following personality traits identified by Adorno:

- Blind allegiance to black-and-white conventional definitions of right and wrong.

- Belief that violence is justified against people who don't agree with conventional definitions of right and wrong, who are different from the individual in question, and who don't submit to conventional authority figures. Seeking such people, condemning and punishing them.

- Strong resistance to new ideas and creativity. Anything less than the conventional is dangerous to "our" society and "our" way of thinking. Belief in simple polemics and answers with no room for other opinions and viewpoints.

- Rigid categorization of everything, including people.

- Obsession with dominant–submissive ways of viewing the world: strong versus weak. Strong adherence to leaders who use uncompromising power to obtain their objectives. Identifying with authority figures. Unrealistic and exaggerated view of personal toughness and strength.

▓   Built-in scapegoating of other groups of people based on internal and typically subconscious feelings of inadequacy and rage. The world is a wild and dangerous place.

2. Homosexuality is a particularly rotten form of delinquency and ought to be severely punished.

If you strongly agree with this statement, then you probably possess the following personality traits identified by Adorno:

▓   Blind allegiance to black-and-white conventional definitions of right and wrong.

▓   Belief that violence is justified against people who don't agree with conventional definitions of right and wrong, who are different from the individual in question, and who don't submit to conventional authority figures. Seeking such people, condemning and punishing them.

▓   Strong resistance to new ideas, creativity, and subjective thinking. Anything less than the tough-minded conventional method is dangerous to "our" society and "our" way of thinking. Belief in simple polemics and answers with no room for other opinions and viewpoints.

▓   Rigid categorization of everything, including people. Stereotyping.

▓   Obsession with dominant–submissive ways of viewing the world: strong versus weak. Strong adherence to leaders who use uncompromising power to obtain their objectives. Unrealistic and exaggerated view of personal toughness and strength.

▓   Built-in scapegoating of other groups of people based on internal and typically subconscious feelings of inadequacy and rage. The world is a wild and dangerous place.

■ Obsession with sex.

3. Every person should have a deep faith in some supernatural force higher than himself to which he gives total allegiance and whose decisions he does not question.

If you strongly agree with this statement, then you probably possess the following personality traits identified by Adorno:

■ Blind allegiance to black-and-white conventional definitions of right and wrong.

■ Strong resistance to new ideas, creativity, and subjective thinking. Anything less than the tough-minded conventional method is dangerous to "our" society and "our" way of thinking. Belief in simple polemics and answers with no room for other opinions and viewpoints.

■ Rigid categorization of everything, including people. Stereotyping. Superstition. Belief that supernatural or mystic things determine our fates.

■ Obsession with dominant–submissive ways of viewing the world: strong versus weak.

4. It is essential for learning or effective work that our teachers or bosses outline in detail what is to be done and exactly how to go about it.

If you strongly agree with this statement, then you probably possess the following personality traits identified by Adorno:

■ Blind allegiance to black-and-white conventional definitions of right and wrong.

■ Strong resistance to new ideas and creativity. Belief in simple polemics and answers with no room for other opinions and viewpoints.

■ Obsession with dominant–submissive ways of viewing the world: strong versus weak. Identifying with authority figures.

5. No matter how they act on the surface, men are interested in women for only one reason.

If you strongly agree with this statement, then you probably possess the following personality traits identified by Adorno:

■ Blind allegiance to black-and-white conventional definitions of right and wrong.

■ Strong resistance to new ideas, creativity, and subjective thinking. Anything less than the tough-minded conventional method is dangerous to "our" society and "our" way of thinking. Belief in simple polemics and answers with no room for other opinions and viewpoints.

■ Rigid categorization of everything, including people. Stereotyping. Superstition. Belief that supernatural or mystic things determine our fates.

■ Obsession with dominant–submissive ways of viewing the world: strong versus weak.

■ Built-in scapegoating of other groups of people based on internal feelings of inadequacy and rage.

■ Obsession with sex.

6. The sexual orgies of the old Greeks and Romans are nursery-school stuff compared to some of the goings-on in this country today, even in circles where people might least expect it.

If you strongly agree with this statement, then you probably possess the following personality traits identified by Adorno:

■ Blind allegiance to black-and-white conventional definitions of right and wrong.

■ Strong resistance to new ideas, creativity, and subjective thinking. Anything less than the tough-minded conventional method is dangerous to "our" society and "our" way of thinking. Belief in simple polemics and answers with no room for other opinions and viewpoints.

■ Obsession with sex.

7. When you come right down to it, it's human nature never to do anything without an eye to one's own profit.

If you strongly agree with this statement, then you probably possess the following personality traits identified by Adorno:

■ Blind allegiance to black-and-white conventional definitions of right and wrong.

■ Strong resistance to new ideas, creativity, and subjective thinking. Anything less than the tough-minded conventional method is dangerous to "our" society and "our" way of thinking. Belief in simple polemics and answers with no room for other opinions and viewpoints.

■ Rigid categorization of everything, including people. Stereotyping.

8. No insult to our honor should ever go unpunished.

If you strongly agree with this statement, then you probably possess the following personality traits identified by Adorno:

- Blind allegiance to black-and-white conventional definitions of right and wrong.

- Belief that violence is justified against people who don't agree with conventional definitions of right and wrong, who are different from the individual in question, and who don't submit to conventional authority figures. Seeking such people, condemning and punishing them.

- Strong resistance to new ideas, creativity, and subjective thinking. Anything less than the tough-minded conventional method is dangerous to "our" society and "our" way of thinking. Belief in simple polemics and answers with no room for other opinions and viewpoints.

- Rigid categorization of everything, including people. Stereotyping.

- Obsession with dominant–submissive ways of viewing the world: strong versus weak. Strong adherence to leaders who use uncompromising power to obtain their objectives. Identifying with authority figures. Unrealistic and exaggerated view of personal toughness and strength.

- Built-in scapegoating of other groups of people based on internal feelings of inadequacy and rage. The world is a wild and dangerous place.

Anyone born into Dauntless may have experienced harsh authoritarian measures while growing up. After all, the initiates coming from other factions are lucky not to die or be seriously injured within days of choosing Dauntless. Bullies abound within Dauntless, and this trait is characteristic of the extremely prejudiced individual (in other words the fascist, if we use Adorno's term).

In addition, each faction—whether Dauntless, Abnegation, Candor, Erudite, or Amity—prefers to remain separate in location, clothes, customs, and mannerisms from the other factions. The Erudite faction constantly issues propaganda against Abnegation and its members. The Erudites go so far as to physically attack members of other factions, wanting them all dead—certainly in the case of the Divergent! This aggressively authoritarian faction definitely displays many traits of Adorno's F-scale. They're hostile to people who belong in different groups.

Another social psychologist, Milton Rokeach, expanded the authoritarian theories beyond the search for fascism and right-wing ideologies. He was born in Poland in 1918, and his family moved to New York when he was seven.[3] In 1973, he published a book called *The Nature of Human Values*,[4] in which he defined the traits in his Rokeach Value Survey. This survey asks people to rank eighteen "terminal" values in order of importance to them, followed by eighteen additional "instrumental" values.

The terminal values refer to the goals that we want to achieve during our lifetimes. The instrumental values refer to the desired behaviors that we think will help us achieve our terminal values.

Rokeach postulated that an individual formulates his attitudes—including ideas about stereotypes, authoritarianism, conventionalism, and so forth—based on these terminal and instrumental values. He found that authoritarian people typically have high levels of prejudice and dogmatism. This corresponds, just as with the F-scale, to the type of behavior and ideology we see in the arrogant and violent leaders (Jeanine and Eric) who are trying to subdue, conquer, drug, and mass-murder people.

The Rokeach terminal and instrumental values tend to vary depending on culture as well as occupations and groups to which we belong. For example, people who are corporate managers have similar Rokeach values, and those who are teachers also display similar values. Community activists have yet a third set of similar values. And so forth. These different sets of values contribute to the conflicts we experience with other groups of people.

What do you think is the major goal, or terminal value, of somebody in Abnegation? Well, we know they are the selfless, that their objective is to "project always outward until [they] disappear," as we're told on page 35 of the bonus materials in *Divergent*. They want to make the world better by serving everyone else. The happiness and well-being of others is primary.

So is the first terminal value, "a comfortable/prosperous life," the primary objective of the Abnegation? No. Does it fit the Amity? No. It doesn't seem to fit the Candor, Dauntless, or Erudite, either.

What about the second terminal value, "an active and stimulating life"? This is not the primary goal of a member of Abnegation, nor does it fit Amity, Candor, or Erudite. However, someone in Dauntless might state that this is her chief goal in life.

The third terminal value is "a sense of accomplishment."

This could be the most important goal in life to an individual in Dauntless or Erudite. In fact, if you stretch the meaning of *accomplishment*, it could fit any faction.

As you work your way through all eighteen terminal values, you can analyze them as above. Some don't seem to fit any of the factions, while others could fit one or multiple factions.

How a person achieves one of these primary goals requires instrumental values, so let's look at a few with the various factions in mind.

If we choose the instrumental value "helpful and working for the welfare of others," this is clearly the way a member of Abnegation tries to achieve her primary goals. If she succeeds, she may have a great sense of accomplishment, for example. Or she may have "inner harmony," which is freedom from inner conflict and another of the terminal values. Or she may have both.

Another instrumental value is defined as "intellect," clearly the way a member of Erudite tries to achieve his primary goals. Yet another is "honesty," which is the method chosen by Candor.

If we look at all eighteen instrumental values, we see that every one of them is a positive attribute. Nowhere do we see a method of living one's life that is along the lines of "killing entire groups of people based on prejudice." This is also true for the terminal values: all are positive. Hence, we must assume that regardless of faction, people believe that they are (*a*) doing what's right and that it is good, and (*b*) their behavior and actions are also what's right and good.

One problem with these value systems and personality tests is that they don't take into account the social environments and historical events that shape a person. Is it enough to evaluate somebody's stated values and his personality traits? Can we safely assume that, based on these personality tests, a person is destined to be a fascist, a prejudiced hatemonger who stereotypes and kills entire populations, a rigid adherent to his own group's way of thinking?

No, we can't, said Yale University Professor Stanley Milgram, who performed a series of famous experiments upon which Veronica Roth says she came up with the idea for *Divergent.*

Milgram wanted to prove that a person doesn't have to come from a harsh, authoritarian home, that he doesn't have to believe in violence as a means to an end, that he doesn't have to be conservative and conventional: such a person can still fall under the control of an authoritarian figure, even a fascist.

One way to look at it is to say a person can be brainwashed into performing a violent or otherwise hateful act. There's an awful of brainwashing going on in *Divergent*: many drugs, many serums, many injected computer devices, total control by the Erudite, and on and on. Remember, Veronica Roth came up with the idea for this series because of the Milgram experiment, which suggested that our moral codes can change given the right conditions.

Milgram began his experiments in 1961, because he was intrigued by World War II criminal Adolf Eichmann's defense that he was responsible for the deaths of millions of Jews only because he was following orders.

Milgram used newspaper advertisements to enlist forty ordinary men, not the types of people whom we typically think of as authority-loving, violent drones . . . or authority-loving, violent Dauntless or Erudite. He was able to persuade these men to inflict what they thought were serious levels of electric shocks to other people.

Here's how it worked:

There were forty Participants, each of whom took the role of a teacher. There were forty Learners, who were accomplices of the psychologists running the experiment. The psychologists told the Learners to react in certain ways and to say certain things to the Participants.

The psychologists told Participant X to give a test to Learner Y. If Learner Y made a mistake, Participant X was required to apply an electric shock. At first, these faked electric shocks—*which Participant X believed were very real*—came in weak doses of 30 volts.

Learner Y begged to be released. Sometimes, Learner Y even told Participant X that he suffered from a heart condition and hence *had* to be released.

The doses increased as the test continued and Learner Y kept making mistakes. At 300 volts, Learner Y would bang the wall and insist that Participant X release him.

The supposed doses reached 450 volts, and the switches on the machines used by Participant X bore labels including such things as DANGER: SEVERE SHOCK and XXX.

After 300 volts, Learner Y refused to respond to anything that Participant X said. He would no longer answer any questions. He sat in stubborn silence.

The psychologists running the experiment now instructed Participant X to inflict another electric shock. Many of the Participants did ask the psychologists if they really needed to continue, but when the answer was yes, they obliged.

Milgram's study showed that an individual can become violent against other people if the level of violence he inflicts increases gradually over time. As the learning test progressed, it was harder and harder for Participant X to withhold the electric shocks. He became committed to giving them, he got used to the action, and the consistency of applying the electric shocks when Learner Y made mistakes egged him on.

In fact, of the forty men used as Participants in the Milgram experiment, twenty-six administered 450-volt electric shocks that were potentially *lethal*. The other fourteen Participants only stopped right before they had to inflict the most dangerous voltage.

Again, in my terminology, you could say that Participant X was brainwashed. He was entrapped into performing increasingly violent behavior.

People can be duped into believing anything. If you grow up in a household where everybody, including your parents, tells you that a certain group of people aren't worthy even to be alive, you could very well grow up to be a highly prejudiced bigot, a believer in authoritarianism and conventionalism. We all know that our world is full of prejudice and stereotypes. Many wars are fought because of these notions, that one group of people somehow doesn't deserve to exist or to be treated humanely. The obvious example is Nazi Germany, but it's by far not the only example. Sadly, this is the view of Jeanine and her Erudite and Dauntless-zombielike followers, that the Divergent are dangerous and need to be identified, captured, subdued, studied like microbes, and eliminated as much as possible. She doesn't think the Amity are worthy of any government leadership, for in her mind, they provide nothing of consequence. She stereotypes everyone: Abnegation are defiled by propaganda just as the Nazis defiled the Jews; Amity are considered worthless. Max— while "brainwashed"—says that Candor is completely worthless because it doesn't provide technology or anything else useful such as security and food.

But who are the Factionless?

At first, we view them much as we think of homeless people. They're impoverished just like the homeless in our society. They live apart from everyone else, just as they basically do in the real world. And just as the real homeless form loose communities amongst themselves, so do the Factionless in the Divergent series.

The Factionless are considered lower than low by most people in Tris's society. Being Factionless is considered a fate worse than death, for as Tris declares very early in *Divergent,* "Without a faction, we have no purpose and no reason to live."

The Authoritarian Personality, which I discussed earlier in this chapter, is the most famous explanation of why people become prejudiced against other groups—one faction against the others, or in this specific case, everybody viewing the Factionless individual as a nameless, faceless, pathetic, stereotyped loser. While various personality tests do point at reasons for prejudice, they tend to be limited in that they downplay situational and societal factors. Prejudice is a lot more than how our brain is wired at birth.

In the real world, people categorize each other all the time—just as they do in *Divergent.* We assume things about people based on their ages, genders, ethnicities, religions, skin colors, sexual preferences, where they live, where they are educated, parents, friends, and so forth.

The world is a complicated place, and for humans to survive, they evolved to organize and sort things, places, events, animals. Even primitive people knew not to eat poisonous plants, and in their brains, this information was most likely categorized in some way. They knew not to go to dangerous territories, where other groups might kill them or where predators might attack them. Even people were sorted into categories, such as family, tribe, enemy, friend, good fighter, mother, man, idiot. This is why human languages evolved to include complex systems of categories that "organize" objects, people, locations, and so forth.

We intuitively *think* we know who is safe and who might not be so safe. If you're lost in a foreign city, do you ask for help with directions and transportation from a guy wearing a hoodie in a dark alley? Or do you ask a cop? Or let's get extreme: Pretend you come from an ordinary or impoverished background and find yourself in a rich neighborhood with no clue how to get back to a main road. You see only two people. One is weeding a rich guy's lawn. The other *is* the rich guy, and he's on his wide veranda, dressed in a white suit with a white summer hat, reading the stock market page of a newspaper, and sipping a martini. Do you ask for help from some rich guy sipping martinis, or do you ask the guy weeding the front lawn? Personally, I'd opt for the guy weeding the lawn. If I happened to be a rich woman dressed in exquisite fashion, heavily invested in stocks, and with a penchant for martinis, I might ask the rich guy.

In short, we typically feel safer with people who remind us of ourselves.

Sometimes this causes great problems, as with the 2012 shooting of seventeen-year-old Trayvon Martin by George Zimmerman in Florida. Off-duty neighborhood watch captain Zimmerman was in a gated community when he saw a young African American man, Trayvon Martin, and called the cops.

Zimmerman told the cops that the unidentified young man seemed to be up to "no good or he is on drugs or something"[5] and also that "these assholes, they always get away."[6]

Zimmerman chased Martin, they fought, and Zimmerman shot and killed Martin only seventy yards from where Martin was staying in the neighborhood. Zimmerman was charged and later acquitted of both second-degree murder and manslaughter. Terrified people in the neighborhood did call the police and reported that someone was screaming for help; but nobody ran outside and stopped the altercation between Zimmerman and Martin, and nobody stopped the man from shooting the boy.

The case made national headlines. Was the shooting a result of racial prejudice? This was the big question in many people's minds. It's true that the dispatcher at the police station first asked Zimmerman "this guy, is he white, black, or Hispanic?"[7] After the acquittal, the U.S. Justice Department announced it was continuing its investigation of civil rights offenses by Zimmerman. Specifically, the Justice Department may bring civil charges against Zimmerman for racially motivated federal hate crimes.[8]

Stereotyping leads to Divergent-like factions. Smart kids tend to hang out together. New Age hippielike people hang out together. Gangs of aggressive bullies roam the subways, spray graffiti, and take risks.

In the United States in 2013, we still have deep-seated stereotyping and prejudices. Many of us may not want to acknowledge it, or perhaps many people are isolated in communities made up of people much like themselves. Hence, they may not have direct contact with bigotry and prejudice. But it still exists against the impoverished, the homeless, the mentally ill, and even against minorities such as Jews, African Americans, Asian Americans, and yes, women.

It's a sad state of affairs. In October 2012, *USA Today* reported that "Racial attitudes have not improved in the four years since the United States elected its first black president," and further that "51% of Americans now express explicit anti-black attitudes. . . ."[9] A 2010 Gallup poll concluded that "43% of Americans admit to feeling at least 'a little' prejudice toward Muslims."[10] According to 2009 FBI hate crime statistics, 71.9 percent of all religious hate crimes in the United States were against Jews.[11] In 2012, the FBI reported that 46.9 percent of hate crimes are based on racial bigotry, 20.8 percent on sexual prejudice, 19.8 percent on religious bigotry, and 11.6 percent on ethnic bigotry.[12] The BBC quoted a U.S. Department of State report in May 2013 that "discrimination against Jews and Muslims is on the rise around the world." In addition, says the BBC, in Egypt, anti-Semites sometimes deny or even glorify the Holocaust, and the Egyptian president has agreed that Jews and their supporters should be destroyed.[13]

An interesting article in *Esquire* quoting national polls dished up 2008 statistics about bigotry in the United States. According to this report, quoting the Pew Research Center, 67 percent of African Americans believe they are "almost always or frequently discriminated against when applying for a job." Also of interest, 38 percent of Asian Americans "believe it's okay for races to live separately" with 35 percent of whites and 33 percent of African Americans agreeing with that statement. The Southern Poverty Law Center reports in this same article that there are 888 hate groups in the United States, including the Ku Klux Klan and neo-Nazis.[14]

I could quote statistics about bigotry and prejudice around

the world for hundreds of pages. I'll conclude with just one more. As of August 30, 2013, the seventeenth Surgeon General of the United States and Distinguished Professor of Public Health Richard H. Carmona, MD, writes that "Today in America, our nation continues to suffer from bigotry based on characteristics such as race, gender, age, sexual orientation, and citizenship status."[15]

By identifying with one group and rejecting others, people lacking confidence feel better about themselves. This is why little kids have "clubs" and exclude outsiders. This is why teenagers join cliques and exclude outsiders. Oddly, this type of behavior continues throughout many people's lives. Old-timers and their buddies in a small religious community might treat outsiders who try to move into their village very poorly. The outsiders might be ostracized and forced to relocate. Whether the community is urban, suburban, or rural, as long as there are at least three people, somebody will be the object of gossip and exclusion.

Groups, or factions, exist to include members and exclude others, the outsiders. After all, you can't be inclusive without being exclusive. Prejudice exists by group members against those who are excluded.

The Factionless are the others, the outsiders. They live separately in very poor circumstances from everyone else. These people are considered losers and underachievers, and people in other factions, if they think about the Factionless at all, view them as drains on critical resources.

While the factions are prejudiced against the Factionless, it is oddly the members of the Factionless who are tolerant with more Divergent-like outlooks. In *Divergent,* Tris notes that the "Factionless, who are supposed to be scattered, isolated, and without community . . . are together." They seem to be their own special faction. And Tris is surprised to see that they are quite "normal" as contrasted to members of the traditional factions. In other words, they laugh, joke, discuss things, they are relaxed with each other, they don't fight. They seem more flexible and open-minded than members of Erudite or Dauntless, don't they? As Edward points out, the Factionless welcomed him. They didn't throw him out based on some arbitrary initiation test or simulation. They seem to embrace everyone. Of course, much later in *Allegiant,* the Factionless are screaming, "Death to the factions" in fits of rage. So perhaps the Factionless really aren't any different from everybody else in this world.

Just as our impoverished do, the Factionless sometimes perform jobs that nobody else really wants, but they earn next to nothing. Society must step in and supply "welfare" of some kind to the Factionless—again, just as in real life—and in the case of the Divergent series, it comes from Abnegation.

We learn from a character named Therese that very few Abnegation fail their initiation tests, so they rarely end up Factionless. It is thought that most Factionless come from the Dauntless faction because they get old and are forced out. But we do eventually learn from Evelyn that many Divergent people are Factionless. After all, individuals who can't curtail their thoughts and ideas are more prone to failing initiations or simply leaving their factions.

In the end, the Factionless unite and rise, and there are a lot of them. While they were the butt of discrimination, now they are the only hope. Unfortunately, they also become enraged in *Allegiant*. Readers are presented with the possibility that, in the end, maybe the Allegiant are correct in thinking that the factions must be restored. I think the Allegiants are incorrect and that the factions are harmful to everybody. The entire scenario points to the overall theme that people inherently are different and that these differences cause us to form alliances and groups. Yet imposed factions force people into holes and stifle freedom of both thought and action. Perhaps we require a balance: enough rules to keep us at bay, but enough freedom to allow us to be human.

PAIN-IN-THE-NECK SIMULATIONS AND SERUMS

Simulations, serums, and injected transmitters are a huge part of the Divergent saga. At times, the simulations are drug-induced, sometimes they occur via electrodes, sometimes they're injected via needles and dart-gun type devices, and at other times, they are induced via tiny computer "transmitters," as the books call them.

From the very beginning, we guess that simulations will play a large part in the story. After all, the first simulation—during the Aptitude Test—determines how Tris and the other kids will spend their lives. If one simulation determines the course of her entire life, then clearly the simulations are vital to the story.

We also guess that some form of drugs will be key to the story and that the drugs are connected somehow to the simulations. We know this because the first simulation occurs via electrodes on Tris's head coupled with a clear liquid that she must drink.

The combination of drugs and electrodes somehow makes her "see" things that are not real. Her entire world becomes like a virtual immersion, in which everything she sees is imaginary. In addition, the simulation includes sounds. For example, a voice tells her to choose between cheese and a knife, dogs snarl at her, nails scrape the floor.

All the senses seem to be engaged by this combination of drugs and electrodes. For example, she feels a dog's breath on her skin, and she even feels its tongue. The sense of smell in the form of cigarettes is present in this sophisticated immersion, too. The only sense that seems to be missing in this first simulation is taste. Overall, this is a highly sophisticated immersion into an imaginary construct.

My guess is that it's the clear liquid, the first "serum," that contains the drugs of the simulation, and the electrodes simply enable Tori to monitor and record Tris's physical body reactions to the hallucinatory immersion. Oddly, Tori also wears electrodes on her head during the simulation. Are we to think that Tori is inside the simulation with Tris, which is how Tori later knows that she must provide a program override?

Questions abound about the Aptitude Test scenario. I'll get to more of them in a minute, but for now, I want to touch only on the matters described above.

First, is it possible for a vial of clear liquid to induce full virtual reality immersion hallucinations that incorporate the senses of sight, sound, touch, and smell?

You most likely know that virtual reality is a term typically confined to computer technology. A virtual reality immersion is a high-tech illusion: computer-generated and lifelike, three-dimensional, and involving the user's senses of sight, sound, touch, and, amazing but true, even smell and taste. While it's not an easy feat to build a system that simultaneously employs all five senses, it can be done. In 2009, scientists created what they called a virtual cocoon, which put a user into an immersion so lifelike that the user couldn't tell whether he was still in reality or immersed in the virtual system. The immersed user had to wear a special headset that resembled a football or motorcycle helmet, and all five senses were active in the virtual state. Professor David Howard of the University of York describes how computerized senses work. "Smell will be generated electronically via a new technique . . . which will deliver a pre-determined smell recipe on-demand. Taste and smell are closely linked but we intend to provide a texture sensation relating to something being in the mouth. Tactile devices will provide touch."[1]

Futurists suggest that within the next few decades, this type of computer technology will fuse with our neural circuitry via nanobots, which are microscopic, computerized machines. These systems will be viewed as an extension to our human minds, and the nanobots—after injection or ingestion—will find their way to the neurons responsible for such things as movement and the senses.

Here's how it might work. The user—for example, somebody like Tris taking her Aptitude Test—swallows a clear liquid that contains these microscopic devices. Another method of delivery is by needle, which we'll discuss later in this chapter.

The nanobots intercept the neurotransmissions, the signals fired from a neuron to other neurons. Anything from the eyes, for example, would be intercepted and suppressed, so the simulation can take over and supply its own neurotransmissions for sight. The devices would suppress smell, sound, taste, and touch in similar ways, supplying different transmissions. For Tris to run, walk, fight, or move in any other way inside the simulation, the nanobots possibly could suppress her real legs and arms from moving in the real world. Then, the bots might trigger her neurons that are responsible for movement so she moves inside the virtual reality simulation. She would hence be moving under the control of the simulation, or she would think that she needs to move and then do so—again, inside the simulation.

A month after the article appeared about the virtual cocoon, noted futurist Ray Kurzweil commented that "go out 10 years [virtual reality immersion is] going to be just about as realistic as real reality."[2] But he added that it'll be twenty to twenty-five years before the nanobots are swarming inside our heads and bodies, triggering the immersion behaviors, conditions, and states. In fact, he described a scenario similar to the one I created above. Nanobots shutting down our biological neurons and creating new signals to correspond to the virtual reality immersions, the simulated environments. He extended the concept dramatically by also suggesting that within these immersions, a woman can virtually be inside the body of her husband, and vice versa, and that millions of characters and environments will be available to people who want to be someone else in any other time in the history or in the future.

Back at the dawn of popular computerization in the 1980s and 1990s, virtual reality was all the rage. Crime shows on television often feature kids addicted to virtual reality–type video games who then went on rampages and killed people. Readers couldn't get enough of novels by writers such as William Gibson, whose startling *Neuromancer* made him akin to a rock star. I know, because I was a huge fan. When I finally met Gibson and he signed a pile of books for me, I was practically buzzing with excitement. Of course, I was still quite young . . . I rarely buzz anymore.

Regardless, I was one of millions of readers who were hooked on virtual reality immersion fiction that was published in the 1990s. It was loosely called cyberpunk.

In the film arena, those of us who couldn't get enough of virtual reality immersions watched the original *Tron* movie and *Blade Runner*: the movie directed by Ridley Scott somewhat based on Philip K. Dick's novel *Do Androids Dream of Electric Sheep?*

I was addicted to and constantly analyzed the 1990s-era *Blade Runner* video game, which was one of the most awesome three-dimensional games of its time. I worked for a year—for free—in exchange for equipment that would enable me to write virtual reality software so I could attempt to create worlds as fascinating as the *Blade Runner* video game. People heralded the *Blade Runner* game as the Next Big Thing. This was in the late '90s, less than fifteen years ago.

Back then, people wished they could go on the *Star Trek: Next Generation* holodeck and have some adventures with the crew. It might seem amusing to teenagers today—does it?—but a short time ago, this was the fantasy of everyone from little kids to teenagers to adults.

In gaming, things didn't progress quickly in terms of virtual reality. Sure, avatar-based three-dimensional games proliferated and became very popular, but they weren't *immersive* virtual reality systems. That is, the gamer wasn't inside his own body experiencing all five senses and running across terrain—it was his avatar that did everything, and typically, anything beyond sight and audio just wasn't in the cards. You could go into an online avatar-based system, but you weren't going to smell the flowers and taste the wine.

Approximately ten years ago, researchers started expressing concern about the future of virtual reality: Would it ever progress to the point where we'd have total immersion? Has interest in immersive simulations declined to the point where all we have is the hype and hope of dreamers and theorists?

I recently popped over to Google Trends (www.google.com /trends/) and searched for "interest over time" in "virtual reality." From a benchmark of 100 that Google applied to this search in 2004, interest has dropped steadily: approximately 60 in 2005, 45 in 2007, 26 in 2009, 15 in 2011—and again these are approximate numbers based on a benchmark—15 in August of 2013.

Just for fun, I also did a Google Trend search for the term "Divergent," and interest in this subject was tipped in the opposite direction, with the benchmark of 100, meaning the time of peak search interest, occurring in 2013.

In 2002, a technology magazine ran an article called, "Whatever Happened to Virtual Reality?" In it, the author, Elizabeth Millard, wrote that the "high cost of the hardware and research and development has discouraged funding." In addition, she noted that "virtual reality appears to have migrated back to originators such as technical universities."[3]

And she was accurate: the costs were too high, and the research returned from commercial to university pursuits.

Virtual reality had flooded us with hype, promising us total immersive experiences that would make gaming better than reality, surgery more affordable, and warfare less likely to kill as many soldiers.

By now, many people are aware that the virtual reality headsets and helmets devised within the past decade cause motion sickness: disorientation, nausea, dizziness. People become physically ill. But this was possibly due to the fact that the computers weren't fast enough to process images in anything but a distorted or choppy manner. Simulator sickness happened because the users' eyes weren't accustomed to anything but real-world speeds. If, for example, you're wearing a virtual reality helmet, the delay in movement—of what you're seeing in the simulation—could force your eyes and inner ears to transmit conflicting signals.

In *Divergent*, serums, and sometimes transmitted signals, alter what people see, hear, taste, smell, and feel, and also how they move. Even a slight variation in timing inside the brain could greatly alter a victim's balance. For example, let's suppose a complex set of signals are required to simulate what Tris sees during a simulation. It could be as simple as the Aptitude Test, in which she's supposedly on the ground with a dog next to her, and she feels the dog's tongue and breath. She hears the dog's nails scrape the floor, and she also hears the dog growling. Although this is the first time the reader witnesses a full-immersion simulation, and it's quite simple compared to many that come later, the Aptitude Test is still extremely complicated. What if the timing's off—by just the slightest amount—between one set of neural interceptions and altered transmissions and the others? So, in this case, what would happen to Tris if she happened to hear the dog growl before the dog appeared, and she happened to feel the dog's breath on her face before she was on the ground? What if the dog's movements weren't exactly in sync with its sounds and

how Tris experiences its breath and tongue? What if the simulation forces her hand to wipe drool off her face, and *then* the
dog shows up and licks her? Any of these scenarios might suffice to distort reality for her to such an extent that she becomes
nauseated, maybe vomits, maybe gets dizzy and passes out,
falls down, can't see clearly, and so forth.

Human balance is greatly affected by the vestibular organs residing in our inner ears. If you're fully immersed in a
simulation that experiences lags—which is quite possible if
commands that alter your senses and movements are transmitted over distances, as they often are in *Divergent*—you
could not only get physically sick, but it's possible that
you also might not be able to stand up, remain stable, and
walk.

Balance means that we can move quickly yet see clearly.
It means we can shift our directions and alter our speeds without problems. It means we are able to orient ourselves correctly with respect to gravity. And finally, it means we can
move freely in a variety of ways, keeping our bodies and the
parts of our bodies stable as we move.

These serums have to be incredibly sophisticated, and I
would argue that they'd have to be rather specific to the individual. Everybody's brain is wired differently. While one person might have a dense set of neurons handling a certain
function, another person might have very few neuronal connections related to the same function.

The wiring just for eyesight can be radically different, hence
requiring different permutations of serums that affect vision.
Some people have weak eyesight, while others don't require
glasses of contact lenses. In fact, some people have eye problems such as glaucoma, cataracts, amblyopia or "lazy eye,"
strabismus or crossed eyes, nystagmus or uncontrollable eye

movements, color blindness, ocular migraines, inflamed optic nerves, or even temporary eye infections and allergies.

The wiring just for hearing can be radically different, as well, requiring alterations in serum drugs for various people. Common conditions that affect our hearing and balance include ear infections, fluid buildup in the ears, injuries due to air or water pressure.

Our ears have outer, middle, and inner parts, and all are employed to enable us to hear sounds. For a serum to change what we hear requires that it process signals coming from the inner part of the ear, the vestibular system, which helps with our spatial orientation, how fast we move, and also our equilibrium. However, what happens if Tris—or some other person who is immersed in a simulation—has a tiny delay in how sound moves from the outer ear to the middle and then to the inner ear? What if one person's ears send these signals in a slightly different timing pattern from somebody else's ears?

For the sake of argument, let's take a case in which a simulation makes all the Dauntless move and speak in the real world as opposed to in a control room. They're like robots or zombies in how they function. If commanded to kill themselves, they do so. If commanded to kill others, they do so. Because they are still in the real world as opposed to inside a control room, the serums and computerization required to alter their brain chemistry must be incredibly complicated and different depending on the individual. Again for the sake of argument, let's say Ms. Dauntless Person is totally under the control of this type of serum. Sound waves travel into Ms. Dauntless Person's outer ears and reach her middle ears, where her eardrum starts to vibrate. In the meantime, let's say the serum has sent nanobots to the neurons in her brain that control what she hears. The nanobots wait for signals from the inner ear. The vibrations in her eardrums travel to her inner ear, which triggers and sends signals to her brain. The inner ear maintains her balance while the nanobots intercept the signals before they reach the "hearing" neurons in her brain. But the timing's off. She just climbed a very tall building in a fierce wind. Her ears are clogged. They're ringing. She can't unplug them. So what she's really hearing on the streets, yelling and gunfire and dogs yowling, and so on, enters her outer ears in muted form. Eventually, the sound is transmitted in signals from her inner ear to these "hearing" neurons, where they are intercepted and replaced with the sounds of a growling Jeanine barking orders. But the real sound waves—the ones in reality as opposed to what Ms. Dauntless Person hears in the simulation—are entering her ears in a choppy fashion, and they're distorted. Hence, it's possible that her brain receives choppy, distorted transmissions, which are intercepted in a choppy, distorted manner. This might result in choppy, distorted replacements of the real sounds with the growling Jeanine barking orders. The signals will be incorrect, the orders unclear. Yet in somebody else, another Dauntless, these same signals might loop through a different highly complex set of neurons, deflect back into a distorted feedback loop, and issue Jeanine's orders over and over again instead of once.

It's puzzling that a serum could contain a method that changes neurons in everybody's brain in identical fashions.

Returning to balance, it depends on far more than what we hear and how we process sounds. Our eyes and muscles are also involved and transmit signals from sensory receptors into our brains. The brain must integrate these signals, from all these additional sources, with the sound signals for us to maintain proper balance. If anything's off, we could stumble, fall, become totally disoriented, get dizzy, pass out, and so forth. This factor yields another complication into how the serums are formulated for different people and how they function.

Christina and all the Dauntless initiates are injected with what I'll call the zombie-Borg serum. Christina is totally under the control of the Erudite, who send her signals to dress, put on holsters, shoot guns, kill people, sleepwalk, march in rhythm, and so forth. She's in the real world, and in the real world, she's still receiving sensory inputs. Her vestibular system regulates her equilibrium and enables her to comprehend, adjust to, and retain her spatial awareness. It also enables her to keep her balance in all ways, no matter what she's doing. It enables her to move without stumbling or falling down. As these signals enter her brain from both sides of her head, the cerebellum maintains and coordinates her balance, movements, and posture, while the cerebral cortex supplies memory and higher-level thinking.

For this type of serum to work, Christina would thus have zombie-Borg serum nanobots sitting at neuronal connections throughout her brain, coordinating all these activities in perfect harmony. From the cerebellum and cerebral cortex, signals are sent to and from the brain stem, which helps identify, sort, and process the sensory information. Also emitted from the cerebellum and cerebral cortex are signals to the vestibulo-ocular reflex, which transmits motor signals that control Christina's eye movements. Now, this is all happening just from the sensory input received from her vestibular system.

A MINI-LOOK AT CHRISTINA

A Candor-born initiate in Dauntless, Christina becomes Tris Prior's best friend. They probably hit it off early in the initiation process because they each understand what the other is going through.

It's difficult for Tris to keep the friendship on track, when while under the "spell" of a truth serum, she admits that she killed Will. Christina had feelings for Will, and the two of them were in a short relationship, so killing Christina's love interest isn't exactly a cool thing to do. It would be hard to kill your best friend's boyfriend and then remain friends with her.

In addition, it sometimes seems as if Christina is jealous of Tris's abilities and strengths. This makes it difficult to keep a strong friendship going, too, because friends shouldn't mind the fact that one is better at sports and activities than the other. But the Dauntless initiation is an unusual situation, and so it makes sense that under the pressure of such extreme life-and-death rituals that Christina would grab a flag won by Tris during the "capture the flag" game.

By the time of *Allegiant*, Christina is a faithful and loyal friend to Tris. For example, during the squirmish with the Factionless, she stops Tris from running into a fight between Edward and an Erudite man. Also, she shoves a woman who elbows Tris in the cheek. And later, when Tris, Uriah, and Christina plan to go outside the fence, Christina puts a calming hand on Tris's shoulder because she knows that her friend is worried about her brother Caleb's execution.

But we're just beginning: we also have to factor in visual sensory inputs and touch into the overall human balance system. The rods and cones in our eyes serve as sensory receptors and transmit impulses to our brains. These transmissions enable the brain to comprehend how an individual is oriented relative to everything and everyone around him, and also enable the brain to adjust this orientation. If these signals are misaligned or incorrect, then Christina could be walking down the street, seeing buildings that appear horizontal rather than vertical, and as she views signs and other objects, they may remain in her field of vision rather than move outside the range of her peripheral vision. How does the serum know that she's suddenly moved from pavement to mud or that a rainstorm has kicked in and messed up her balance and ability to run?

Sensory input related to balance also reaches the brain from our muscles, skin, blood vessels, and joints. The body also uses these inputs to regulate our heart and respiratory rates, body temperatures, blood pressure, and reflexes. If Christina leans against a wall, sensory receptors in the heels of her feet are triggered. If she holds a rifle in her hand, sensory receptors in her fingers and palm send signals to her brain. If the terrain changes from smooth pavement to rocky mud, her ankles transmit signals so her brain knows how to maintain her balance under these different conditions. Think about it. Something happens when you're running on a flat, dry surface as opposed to when you're running in the rain over slick mud. Your brain knows and adjusts your balance and your movements.

If any of the signals just mentioned conflict with one another, Christina's balance could be totally thrown off. Sometimes, if you stand near an elevator, your stomach drops and you feel a bit dizzy. It's as if you're moving rather than the elevator. Sometimes, you see something flash past you, and for a moment, it creates the illusion that you are moving instead. For that moment, you become disoriented. While these sensory systems are off balance, your muscles, skin, and joints send signals to your brain that you are actually *not* moving. Then your cerebellum and cerebral cortex let you know that this doesn't make sense, that this has happened to you before, that you are actually not moving, and this enables you to shift your eyes from the rapidly moving object, hence restoring your balance by making your eyes receive sensory input that you are standing still.

All these highly complex systems contribute to our balance, and all must be coordinated with perfect timing and precision in each individual for the serum to work correctly. Also keep in mind that I'm providing a very simple view of these processes and that while neuroscientists have made huge strides, there's an enormous amount that we don't know.

If we knew how our brains really function to the level required for a zombie-Borg serum to function in thousands of people, we would know how to cure such things as manic depression, amyotrophic lateral sclerosis, all sorts of neurotic behaviors, psychotic breaks, and so forth.

SENSORY SYSTEMS: REALITY VERSUS PERCEPTION

A simple way of viewing overall sensory systems is to say that in most cases, (1) the body receives a physical stimulus, (2) a series of actions transduces the stimulus into a variety of nerve impulses constituting a message, and (3) the brain responds to the message with an inner representation of the sensory inputs or a perception of what has happened and what it means.

Jeanine's use of magnetic resonance imaging (MRI) on Tris's brain is on target. This is one method that scientists use in the real world to examine our brain functions.

Sensory receptor cells transduce, or convert energy from one form to another. They convert external stimuli into light energy, chemical energy, sound energy, or mechanical energy. The cell then forms a voltage known as a receptor potential.

Vision, sound, smells, and tastes are actually mental constructions, or perceptions, created by our brains. For example, our sensory receptors input electromagnetic waves that have different frequencies, and our brains *perceive* these waves as colors. When we hear words and music, we're actually receiving sensory inputs that are pressure waves. When we smell cigarettes, as Tris does in her Aptitude Test, what's really happening is that our brains have *interpreted* chemical inputs in the air as the smell of cigarettes. The same is true of taste: these are chemicals that trigger our *perceptions* of taste.

If we think about the fact that our senses are really just perceptions internal to our brains, then it might be possible to adjust or replace our perceptions as with the *Divergent* simulations and serums. The direct sensory inputs wouldn't necessarily be key to the process. After all, what I perceive might be quite different from what you perceive—and we might be receiving identical sensory inputs. I might taste sugar and enjoy it; you might taste sugar and spit it out. Somebody else might enjoy the taste of vinegar and enjoy the taste of whole limes. What I view as a shade of purple, you might see as a shade of burgundy or dark red. My gray might not equal your gray. Hence, what an individual perceives is not an accurate record of reality. It's an internal construct in his brain. And that internal construct is based on his own wiring.

The only time this seems radically difficult and bizarre is when the *Divergent* serums and computerization work in real-world constructs as opposed to enclosed, controlled, simulation rooms. For example, if Tris is confined to a room under a controlled environment—in a chair and not moving through the real world, with no street noises or people in reality talking to her, with no real dogs barking, with no city smells or body odors hitting her, with no walking or running in reality, and so on—then it might be easier to make her brain simulate an immersive reality. Once the immersion is in the real world, then the serum and computerization must intercept, interpret, and replace real-world sensory inputs and responses. That's much more complicated.

When a stimulus excites a sensory cell in our bodies, the cell transmits a signal through a delicate nerve fiber into the brain. Different types of receptors handle different types of sensory inputs. In the human body, we can summarize the various types of sensory receptors as follows:

- **Sight.** Photoreceptors called rods and cones receive and are stimulated by light.
- **Smell.** Chemoreceptors, our olfactory sense neurons, receive and are stimulated by chemicals.
- **Taste.** Chemoreceptors, our taste buds, receive and are stimulated by chemicals.
- **Sound.** Mechanoreceptors that are cochlear hair cells receive and are stimulated by air pressure waves.
- **Touch.** Mechanoreceptors, thermoreceptors, nociceptors, and chemoreceptors known as dorsal root ganglion neurons receive mechanical, thermal, and chemical stimuli.

These various types of receptors have specific organizations and sizes.

Rods respond to single photons and are able to detect low levels of light. Cones respond to hundreds of photons.

They are also packed in denser formations than rods and respond more quickly to sensory inputs. Cones receive red, blue, and green light, enabling the brain to determine the colors that a person is viewing. In extremely simple terms, color perception involves subtracting the response from one color-sensitive cone from the responses of other sets of other color-sensitive cones. The retina, which resides in the back of the eye, also has photoreceptors.

When an odor combines with an olfactory receptor in the nose, something called a G protein is activated. The body continually degrades and replaces olfactory cells because they are constantly exposed to chemical odors from the environment. While visual sensory receptors handle three primary colors, your nose has approximately two thousand olfactory sensory receptors. Each type detects a specific chemical odor. Unlike rods and cones, the olfactory receptor cells are bipolar with one end having the actual odor receptor proteins in the nose cilia and the other having a long axon that sends signals to the brain. On the ends of the nose cilia are specialized receptor proteins for particular odors. Each type of receptor recognizes an odor based on factors such as its lipid solubility and its vapor pressure, and if the receptor is stimulated, the G protein activation occurs. I will leave the discussion of G proteins for another time because the science is well beyond the scope of this particular book.

Our gustatory system contains sensory receptors for many chemicals that lead to perceptions of five tastes: sweet, sour, salty, bitter, and what is known as umami, a savory sort of flavor. Taste is quite complicated, and for the purposes of this book, I'll simplify everything as much as possible.

The receptor sensors are on microvilli on the tips of taste

cells. There are approximately 50 to 150 receptor cells per taste bud, and your tongue, mouth, and even your throat have thousands of taste buds. As with the olfactory sensory cells, the taste sensory cells also have a limited lifespan. The body switches off the taste receptor cells because they're exposed to external chemicals.

The transduction process of the sensory receptor differs depending on the type of taste. For example, salt receptor cells open sodium channels, and sodium ions depolarize the receptor cell.

The detection of sweet tastes happens when G protein receptors are activated and something called cAMP is formed, closing a potassium channel. This action depolarizes the receptor cell.

For a sour taste, detection depends on the pH of a potassium channel, which then closes, hence depolarizing the receptor cell.

The bitter taste is more complex. In short, it increases calcium in the receptor and involves the activation of a variety of chemicals.

Finally, in short, the umami taste receptors detect the presence of glutamate.

The auditory system, as described elsewhere in this chapter, encodes pressure waves that vary in frequency, or pitch, and amplitude, or loudness. Our auditory sensory receptors, which line the cochleas of the inner ears, process events every ten- to fifteen-millionths of a second. The hair cells, or cilia, inside the ear, bend as sound waves pass, and this alters the pressure on and tension of mechanoreceptor channels, which are open or closed. Placement of the hair cell is key to many of its special properties, so for example, a hair cell near the top surface of the basilar membrane responds to low frequencies and a hair cell near the bottom surface responds to high frequencies.

Touch is handled by a variety of sensory cells, including somatosensory receptors in the skin such as nociceptors for handling pain and thermoceptors for handling temperatures. Also included are sensory receptors in the muscles, bones, joints, internal organs, and elsewhere.

The somatosensory system is quite different from the sensory systems that enable us to smell and taste, and so forth. Three somatosensory pathways exist in the spinal cord, and each has a different target in the brain.

One pathway is for discriminative touch and enables us to process what we feel on our skin, including pressure and vibrations. This pathway also enables our brain to perceive the shape and texture of an object that we are not viewing.

The second pathway is for pain and temperature, and it also handles what happens when we're itching or somebody is tickling us.

The third pathway is called proprioception, and its sensory receptors handle things we may not be aware of that occur beneath our skin and inside our bodies, things such as stretching our muscles and putting pressure on our joints and tendons. This pathway targets the cerebellum, which requires constant feedback about our muscles.

Along with sensory simulation factors, the Aptitude Test includes computer programming that takes different paths based on Tris's choices, for example, cheese versus a knife. Eventually, by a process of elimination, the software concludes the faction for which a teenager is best suited. Of course, for Tris and other Divergents, the software apparently concludes that the subject has aptitude for multiple factions. These results are called "inconclusive."

If this were not sophisticated enough, the software also enables another person—such as Tori, who operates the simulations—to alter the actual simulation while it's running. In Tris's case, this real-time alteration of the software pops Tris on a bus. Tori does this "on the fly." This is called a "program override." Caleb, who researched Aptitude Test design, explains that the operators aren't even taught how to perform a program override when the subject shows aptitude for three factions. Possibly the reason is because, as Eric says elsewhere in the *Divergent* book, most Divergent obtain two results in the Aptitude Test, and Tris is the only one he knows who obtained three results. This means of the personality traits of Peace-Love-Kindness, Selflessness, Honesty, Bravery, and Intelligence, only one person has ever displayed three. It's a bit difficult to imagine that an Abnegation, for example, who is Selfless, might not also be Intelligent, full of Peace-Love-Kindness, and maybe even Honest or Brave. How is it possible to be Selfless without having some of these other attributes?

And here's another wrinkle to the Aptitude Test. While the software eliminates one faction after another and supposedly yields a result that places a teen in only one faction, this is not the only way a result occurs. If the teen is suited for more than one faction, the software does not have the built-in artificial intelligence necessary to place the subject into a particular faction. This apparently is when a program override is necessary.

Instead, the simulation ends, and the operator, Tori, arrives at the conclusion. It's the operator who decides, for example, that Tris has "equal" aptitude for Dauntless, Abnegation, and Erudite. And Tori is a volunteer Aptitude Test operator, not an expert, with her other occupation being a tattoo artist.

As an aside, Tori originally discovers Tris's Divergence and warns her to be very careful. Despite the fact that the knowledge could lead to her own downfall, Tori is selfless in that she keeps Tris's Divergence a secret. Much later in *Allegiant,* when Tris sees Tori's corpse, Tris is filled with sadness because she's grateful to Tori for helping her see that she could leave the Abnegation faction.

Whether we really reach full virtual reality immersion in the next twenty years or so is debatable. Will real immersion always require headsets that can make us dizzy? If so, then the world of *Divergent* is so far into the future that the very nature of what defines us as human will be debatable. By then, we'll be enhanced with genetic modifications and microscopic devices, as well as neural implants and nanobots.

Jeanine has created all sorts of serums, which I loosely think of as injected liquids containing drugs and—it is my guess—nanobots of some kind. In addition, other factions use serums, as well. For example, the Amity brainwash people using a peace serum.

Will nanobot technology be sophisticated enough to deliver drugs to our neural systems and alter our conscious states? While I'll delve into drug delivery via nanobots later, for now, let's look at the types of drugs that might be powerful enough to induce hallucinations, alter the senses, and force bodies to move in specific ways.

Humans have been seeking out and consuming mind-altering drugs throughout recorded history. We know that people three thousand years ago in ancient Babylon imbibed alcohol in special drinking houses. People have been smoking marijuana for thousands of years, as well, both in India and in the Arab world. The ancient Incans and Peruvian Indians chewed coca leaves to help them weather life in high altitudes where food was scarce and strength was needed.

A BRIEF HISTORY OF DRUGS

A drug is a chemical substance used to either treat illnesses or provide pleasure and relief. By trial and error, hunter-gatherers long ago learned which plants were poisonous, which were useful as food, which were able to treat illnesses, and which were able to provide pleasure and relief. This type of information was handed down from one generation to the next, until eventually, a person with this knowledge became known as a shaman, witch doctor, or medicine man. Typically, the witch doctor combined magical and religious rites with his knowledge of medicinal plants.

The role of witch doctor was one of power. After all, people were highly superstitious and believed that the spirits or gods could destroy crops at whim, cause famines, illnesses, plagues, floods, attacks, and even death. Diseases and death were acts of the gods or spirits. Demons and supernatural spells caused serious illness and death. The supernatural could suck the souls out of people. It was the witch doctor's job, among other things, to heal sick people and help relieve pain using medicinal plants. He had to extract the evil entity, the supernatural that had sucked out the soul from a person's body. He had to then employ his own spells and incantations, along with potions and other medicinal concoctions, and heal the person. And perhaps, it was thought, he could also intervene and keep the gods and spirits on the side of the people.

In the second century A.D. during the Han dynasty, the

Chinese published the book *Shen-Nung Pen T'Sao Ching,* which identified 365 medicinal plants. During the Ming dynasty in the sixteenth century, Li Shin Chen overhauled the ancient book, calling the new version the Great Pharmacopoeia, *Pen T'sao Keng Mu.* In this version were 1,898 medicines that originated from a variety of sources, including plants, animals, and minerals. Li Shen Chen studied how various medicines interacted and is commonly considered the first scientifically oriented pharmacologist in recorded history.

However, even in modern times, pharmacology in China differs greatly from how drugs are prescribed in the United States and other Western societies. As with the medicine men of old, many Chinese remedies are complex mixtures that rely on not only science but also philosophical ideas. It could be said that Chinese medicine is an art as well as a science, whereas in the West, doctors prescribe specific chemical substances to treat illnesses, and philosophical ideas don't come into play.

The ancient Indian system called ayurveda is several thousand years old. As with Chinese drugs, ayurvedic pharmacology relies on complex mixtures of natural drugs. The ancient Egyptians also prescribed a wide variety of plant-based medicines.

Because nobody in the Divergent series seems to be Chinese or Indian in background, I suppose whatever medicines they might be taking would not interact with the mind-altering drugs forced on people by the Erudite and other faction leaders. Should someone from another cultural background show up, the interactions of all the serums with normal medicinal remedies could cause vomiting, insanity, death—who knows? In fact, this is true even for those people of ordinary Western-society background: the drugs taken for true medicinal reasons probably would interact strongly and in bad ways with the massive amounts of heavy drugs used by the faction leaders to control people and force them into immersive simulations.

In Greece in A.D. 55, Diosorides published *De Materia Medica,* which stood as the pharmaceutical bible for more than a thousand years. Also, Hippocrates began what is now thought of as the scientific approach to medicine. In A.D. 60 in Rome, Pliny published *Natural History,* which identified and described natural medicinal remedies.

The use of herbal drugs was widespread in Europe, and Nicholas Culpeper in the 1600s published the astrological herbal-remedy tome, *Pharmacopoeia.* Still, notions persisted that the shape or color of a leaf, for example, might be related to its medicinal use. To list one example, medical doctor John Brown in eighteenth-century Edinburgh claimed that only two drugs were necessary, alcohol and opium.[4] What's interesting about Brown's ideas is that he practiced medicine at a time when Edinburgh was filled with poverty, smallpox, cholera, typhus, and typhoid. And indeed, "one of the most common conditions Scottish physicians had to contend with was delirium tremens,"[5] which results from extreme alcoholism.

It wasn't until true scientific medicine evolved that remedies shifted dramatically from the mythological and supernatural merged with herbs to an approach based on *only drugs.* Louis Pasteur is famous for not only pasteurizing milk but also inoculating people for rabies, cows and sheep for anthrax, and chicken for cholera. Then in 1865, the surgeon Joseph Lister reduced infections and death during surgeries when he started placing antiseptic barriers between wounds and the open air. William Morton, who was a dentist, introduced ether as an anesthetic during surgeries and childbirth. Then back in Edinburgh, James Young Simpson in 1847 discovered that chloroform could be used as a superlative anesthetic during surgeries.

In nineteenth-century Germany, scientists isolated pure medicinal chemicals from plants for the first time. In 1803, they isolated morphine from opium and used it to relieve pain. Physician Paul Ehrlich's studies of body tissues and chemicals led to the modern concept that receptors in our bodies have affinities for specific drugs.

Fast-forward to today. Sales of medicinal drugs in the United States alone are in the hundreds of billions. *The New York Times* places the figure at $325.7 billion in 2012.[6] And these are prescriptions. They don't take into account the sales of illegal drugs.

Psychoactive drugs are probably the type used in the Divergent series to alter states of consciousness and impose auditory, visual, and other sensory changes in an individual's brain. This type of drug could also change how somebody in *Divergent* perceives objects and other people; so for example, when Jeanine creates a new serum to change Tobias's surroundings to manipulate his will, she might very well be using some form of psychoactive drugs. This would also be the case with Amity's peace serum that they can bake into their bread. Even the purple paralytic serum and the death serum, as described by Peter, could be psychoactive drugs. It is indeed possible to produce paralysis using drugs that work on the nervous system.

Our consciousness depends on the intricate network of more than ten billion neurons in our brains. If you think ten billion is a big number, then consider that the number of connections among the neurons is thousands of times more. As I've mentioned earlier, targeting neurotransmissions and specific neurons and groups of neurons for drugs in a system this complicated would require a feat of incredible science. But lest you think I'm a naysayer, let me also mention that I do believe given our current neuroscientific progress that in the future, it may be possible to do many of these things to our own brains.

The ten billion neurons and their interconnections in the brain are referred to as the central nervous system. As the network continues into the spinal cord and body, it's known as the peripheral nervous system. All neurons in the central nervous system interact using only one method, neurotransmitters where the neurons overlap at the synapses.

Psychoactive drugs in the real world typically mimic or change the release of these neurotransmissions. This is the same idea as what happens in the Divergent series. Earlier, I gave you a quick overview of how the nervous system works. Psychoactive drugs bind like endogenous neurotransmitters to one or more receptors.

If a drug binds to a receptor and creates the same response as happens naturally with an endogenous neurotransmitter, then the drug is called an agonist. If on the other hand, the drug binds to the receptor yet creates no response, then it's known as an antagonist or blocker. A psychoactive drug used in an immersive simulation probably works to some extent as an antagonist, blocking normal neurotransmissions. Sometimes these antagonists actually do fit with a receptor even better than the normal neurotransmitter yet still block the normal response. Scientists today aren't always sure how this happens; possibly, the drug fits into the receptor site but not perfectly enough to enable ion channels to open or trigger G proteins.

The *Divergent* drugs, of course, also must replace neurotransmissions with new ones, which most likely involve different neuronal subsets of the complex networks.

I do wonder why nobody in *Divergent* has developed a serum to combat the effects of the evil serums. If this much is known about brain chemistry and drug interactions at the neuronal level, then surely somebody in Erudite could create antidotes. The level of brain research required to create the serums is so significant that multiple people and research teams would have to be involved on some level. A lot of people would know how to create these serums. Science in the real world doesn't function in a vacuum, a single laboratory with a single genius laboring away day and night and injecting himself repeatedly with mysterious preliminary drugs. But in the world of *Divergent*, society has collapsed, so we can safely assume that the real-world methods of science are no longer valid. Here, a handful of geniuses who are also evil and/or maniacally insane could slave away in pseudo-solitude and devise these horrible serums. But even they would have to document their research, wouldn't they? Otherwise, they wouldn't be able to keep track of the incredible complexities involved in developing so many psychoactive drugs. All it would take is one ethical and moral Erudite to get that documentation, reverse engineer or otherwise revise the drug creation methods, and produce untested antidotes.

Which brings us to another point: On whom do the Erudite test these incredibly dangerous psychoactive serums? How many people have died in this research, and why don't the more ethical and moral Erudite know about the deaths?

In *Allegiant,* we learn that Jeanine Matthews did indeed test her fear serum by injecting it into a Factionless man. In exchange for letting her tamper with his brain and scare the hell out of him, he received food and clothing. While we're told that he was never the same after Jeanine's experiments, we can guess what this means: that she permanently mangled his brain. My guess is that she must have performed these types of experiments on a lot of luckless people. How she hid the experiments remains a mystery.

These are just ideas to think about related to *Divergent,* and truly, the mark of a great work of science fiction is that it seems as if it could happen someday. Dissecting and analyzing both the science and the societies in science fiction is both fascinating and instructive. It certainly adds to the enjoyment of the series to think about the neuroscience of this world.

Sometimes, an agonist and an antagonist compete at a receptor site, and the response is based loosely on their concentrations. Sometimes, a drug has an immensely large concentration of an agonist, but even so, the drug cannot compete against the responses produced by an antagonist because the agonist and antagonist are actually binding to slightly different sites.

An example might be the purple paralytic serum that Peter mentions. It reminds me of the South American arrow poison that contains tubocurarine, which the indigenous Indians would pack into hollow bamboo tubes. This form of curare was used to paralyze prey by stopping the contraction of the animal's respiratory muscles. Tubocurarine will not paralyze or kill you if ingested in correct doses in pill form, for example, but it is toxic if injected in sufficient doses. The reason is that the tubocuranine compounds cannot pass through the digestive tract lining into the bloodstream. If injected directly into the bloodstream, tubocurarine can paralyze a victim within one minute. It basically blocks the acetylcholine receptor site between a motor neuron and muscle, meaning it is an antagonist at the acetylcholine receptor site. In addition, it blocks the ion channel gated by the receptor.

If a moral and ethical Erudite wants to create an antidote—assuming the paralytic serum contains tubocurarine, that is—it will be difficult. Nicotine is an example of a powerful agonist that works at the same site between a motor neuron and muscle as tubocurarine. However, no matter how much nicotine is present, the antagonistic paralytic poison will prevail, and the victim will remain paralyzed, though perhaps not so badly.

Examples of what are called inverse agonist drugs are Valium and Halcion, which bind to the benzodiazepine receptor site and modulate a GABA (the main central nervous system inhibitory neurotransmitter gamma-aminobutyric acid) ion channel to allow chloride ions to flow more readily into the neuron, thus hyperpolarizing the neuron. This sedative effect in the central nervous system relaxes people and reduces their anxiety.

Complicating the delivery of psychoactive serums that not only alter neurotransmitter receptor sites but change the overall chemical transmission is the fact that the same neurotransmission can have different forms of receptors. In short, various receptors are divided into subclasses.

Due to differences in the sequences of their amino acid components, one subclass may have a different ability to bind drugs than another subclass. A common example is the cholinergic receptor, for which subclasses N1 and N2 respond to nicotine and subclasses M1 and M2 respond to the toxic mushroom alkaloid called muscarine.

A receptor's three-dimensional structure dictates the neurotransmitters or drugs that can bind to it. You can think of the amino acid sequence as the structure of a lock—the receptor for which only certain keys, neurotransmitters and drugs, fit.

Because of these differences and subclasses, two drugs may have the same overall mechanisms but differ greatly in the number and type of side effects they cause in different people. An SSRI antidepressant drug, for example, may have the same serotonin mechanism as another SSRI antidepressant. However, there are various serotonin receptor subclasses, and each antidepressant drug may interact with them in different ways. This causes the two drugs to affect people in a wide variety of ways and to produce different side effects.

The major neurotransmitters that *Divergent* psychoactive drugs might intercept or induce include acetylcholine, dopamine, norepinephrine, GABA, glycine, serotonin, endorphins, histamine, and adenosine.

I've already mentioned acetylcholine, which is the main neurotransmitter of motor neurons in the peripheral nervous system as well as the neurotransmitter of many central nervous system neurons in the basal ganglia and motor cortex. In addition to such things as the paralytic actions of tubocurarine, nerve gases inactivate acetylcholinesterase, which destroys acetylcholine. This might seem counterproductive on the surface because it's basically the opposite of what tubocurarine does—remember, tubocrarine blocks acetylcholine stimulation and hence paralyzes its victim. Nerve gases that inactivate acetylcholinesterase are deadly because without acetylcholinesterase, the neuron uncontrollably produces acetylcholine, causing respiratory failure.

Studies show that a network of neurons functioning with dopamine are key to reward mechanisms in the brain. Habit-forming drugs probably enhance dopamine release or act on neurons in other ways that affect dopamine production. For example, we know that cocaine blocks the reuptake of dopamine from synapses. We also know that amphetamines trigger the release of dopamine into the synapses. Opiates, barbiturates, and benzodiazepines encourage dopamine production by lowering the thresholds required to activate it.

When the Dauntless traitors are shot up with zombie-Borg serum, as I call it, they shuffle in unison with frozen faces. They are indeed like zombies, responding only to the commands of their "masters." Well, we know that inadequate dopamine transmission in the substantia nigra produces symptoms of Parkinson's disease, which happen to include a shuffling walk and frozen face. Could it be that the serum used on the Dauntless traitors works in a similar way to Parkinson's disease? If so, it's a very sophisticated drug. Not only does it zombify a person, but it can also make all the zombified people march in unison and perform other actions as if everybody's in a chorus line. Or it can make only one person—or two, or any other subset of people—perform a specific set of actions. In addition, the "masters" can issue commands to one person, a set of people, or all zombified people at once.

When you consider how many subclasses, or types, of each neurotransmitter exist and all the permutations of how drugs interact with them, it's amazing that the Erudites have been able to create this zombie-Borg (as I call it) drug. Dopamine has five types of receptor subclasses!

Norepinephrine is found in most sympathetic nerves, as well as in the hypothalamus and in other neurons in the central nervous system. The sympathetic nervous system strongly affects whether we fight when attacked or run, which is commonly called "fight or flight." In part, it is responsible for our reactions to fear: increased heart rate, increased blood pressure, dilation of our pupils, and increased sweating. Amphetamines act indirectly on norepinephrine, serotonin, and dopamine synaptic sites. The *nor* in *norepinephrine* implies that nitrogen in the molecule is missing a methyl or other alkyl group. Without getting into enormous amounts of chemistry, we can also say that if the nitrogen has a methyl group, then it is called epinephrine, which is another name for adrenaline. When we're experiencing extreme physical or mental stress, our adrenal glands release this hormone.

With serum knowledge, the Dauntless leaders could have enhanced the norepinephrine and epinephrine in Al's nervous system, thus enabling him to handle fear better. In fact, rather than subject Dauntless "recruits" to the rigorous and deadly initiation tests and simulations, an intelligent Dauntless leader could instead inject some enhanced brew of norepinephrine and epinephrine into the young initiates.

GABA, mentioned earlier, is found in the basal ganglia and cerebellum, and among the drugs that act at the GABA synapses are alcohol, barbiturates, and benzodiazepines. The GABA neurotransmitter has two types of receptor subclasses.

Drugs such as PCP bind to receptor sites related to glycine, glutamic acid, and aspartic acid, which are some of the amino acid neurotransmitters in the spinal cord, the cortex, and the cerebellum. This type of neurotransmitter is involved in strokes and possibly epileptic seizures.

Serotonin, which I touched upon earlier, is the neurotransmitter that operates in a restricted area of the brain called the raphe nuclei. Interestingly, if the serotonin is in the pineal gland, then it transforms into the skin pigmentation hormone called melatonin. And also interesting, melatonin is sold over the counter as a sleep aid because it contributes to our sleeping and waking cycle. Among the drugs that operate at serotonin synapses are antidepressant SSRIs, as well as drugs that suppress appetite and the psychedelic drug LSD. Serotonin has fifteen types of receptor subclasses. Again, we can only marvel at the precision with which the Erudite drugs work. Nobody accidentally gets a sudden very deep tan or complexion when eating Amity bread. Nobody accidentally dozes off. Nobody accidentally has a psychotic break and starts hallucinating, hearing things, or thinking he's Jesus or Satan. It's remarkable, really, especially when you also consider that drugs affect people in different ways and also that the Amity might have built up a tolerance to their own peace serums, whereas somebody like Tris getting smacked with a heavy dose would not have any tolerance at all. Do they supply their children with small amounts of peace serum, then increase the dose as time goes by until as old folks, they have to eat twelve loaves of peace-bread three times per day?

These are all ideas to ponder. In a novel, the writer can't get into all the details of the science behind the story. If she does, the story will get mired in detail and lose its impact. Nobody wants to read a novel that's basically a textbook! So writers tend to leave many details to their readers' imagination, and in the case of hard science fiction, we have the pleasure of analyzing the futuristic science and trying to discover how it might unfold in the real world.

Endorphins increase our states of relaxation, calm, and dreaminess. Drugs such as morphine and heroin increase the amount of endorphins released in our body. Endorphins have four types of receptor subclasses.

Histamines can sedate a person, as evidenced by anybody who swills cold medicines that can knock you out or make you dizzy.

Adenosine, which helps make us feel tired, is the final neurotransmitter that I'll briefly describe. It is found in all cells in the body and as an injectable pharmaceutical drug, it is available as an odorless, white powder that is soluble in water. It regulates the body's normal cycle of being alert and becoming lethargic.

When you drink coffee, the caffeine is seen by your brain receptors as if it is adenosine. Hence, the real adenosine does not lock into the receptors. However, the increase in your brain's activities makes the adrenal glands crank out more adrenaline than normal, keeping you more alert. This is how the caffeine in coffee helps you stay awake and work longer hours.

It's possible that Amity's peace drug is a form of marijuana, which after all, can be baked into breads and makes a person feel happy. The peace-loving, fun-loving Amity don't seem to have much anxiety, just like someone taking marijuana, and they do laugh and giggle a lot (and eat a lot of those baked goods).

In terms of hallucinatory drugs in real life, they cannot be injected in order to induce specific hallucinations in people. There's no way for somebody to force LSD into another person in order to make him face the three worst fears of his life, choose between cheese and a gun, or whatever.

Other than lysergic acid diethylamide (LSD), other hallucinogens include mescaline, psilocybin, and dimethyltryptamine (DMT). The hallucinations can indeed include types used in the *Divergent* immersive simulations: vision, sound, taste, touching something that doesn't exist. If the Erudite can harness hallucinogens in extremely precise ways, then it's possible to induce the types of simulations in the *Divergent* world, but this type of specificity is way beyond current knowledge.

Most of the serums are injected into a person's neck in the

world of *Divergent*. Not always, but usually. Injections of serums and transmitters occur a lot in this world, and the injection sites are typically on a person's neck. It seems likely that
someone like Tris or Four would eventually have problems accepting additional injections.

In the late 1800s and the first decade of the 1900s, the
physician Paul Ehrlich came up with the idea of "magic bullets" that would target and destroy specific germs in a person's body without hurting anything else. In 1909, Ehrlich
with collaborator Sahachiro Hata discovered a drug called
Salvarsan that helped destroy syphilis infections. This was the
first "magic bullet."

Today, we have magic bullets in a variety of sizes and
shapes, all extremely small, of course. The nanoparticles, which
can be considered magic bullets, deliver drugs as liposomes,
dendrimers, micelles, nanoemulsions, and nanosuspensions.

Nanoparticles themselves are stable, colloidal particles that
are ten to one thousand nanometers in diameter. As delivery
mechanisms, they contain the actual drugs dissolved or
trapped in a polymer lipid solution or on the surface of the
nanoparticle.

In the real world, research into nanoparticle delivery of
drugs has progressed at a phenomenal rate during the past few
decades. Both universities and corporations have facilitated
this boom in nanoparticle-delivery research.

Because nanoparticles are so small, they can infiltrate tumor tissues and target cancerous areas that microparticles
cannot target. The drug nanoparticles are dispersed more
widely in the body.

They also have the potential to permeate the blood–brain
barrier, which is highly impermeable. The most effective way
to treat brain diseases is to target and then supply medicines

to specific areas—even specific receptors—of the brain. Among the scientists working in this field are a team at the Department of Pharmaceutics of the University of Minnesota, who published a paper in 2004, in which they suggested that insulin-like growth factors applied to the nasal passages can bypass the blood–brain barrier and "rapidly elicit biological effects at multiple sites within the brain and spinal cord."[7]

A company called Nanospectra Bioscience (at www.nano spectra.com) sells nanoparticles with specific optical properties to medical research institutions. They are also working on nano-sized "AuroShell particles" that may help in treating brain tumors. However, after injecting these particles, a doctor will have to focus a near-infrared laser on the tumor. The particles will then absorb and convert the wavelength of the laser light into heat, which will help destroy the tumor. Note that while this is clinical research, it does involve injecting nanoparticle drugs into a person's body, and those drugs do migrate into a specific area of the brain. If you push this type of technology far into the future, you can perhaps see the potential of how the *Divergent* serums are dispersed into the brain and how they target specific combinations of neural receptors.

Because nanoparticles can target specific sites in the body more efficiently, using them for drug delivery tends to mitigate the harmful dose-related toxicities as well as harmful side effects.

Current scientific research into bio-applications of nanoparticles use various methods to deliver the medicines. It's possible that the serums in *Divergent* are actually nanoemulsions, which contain one liquid distributed as droplets in another liquid. For example, droplets with fatty acids on their surfaces can be dispersed in water. If the droplets are of nano-size, the result is a nanoemulsion. This is useful if a drug is not particularly soluble.

To increase a drug's solubility, scientists can reduce the size of the drug molecules, making them into drug nanocrystals. Although the overall size is smaller, this technique supplies a bigger surface area for each particle and improves its solubility in water. This might be another technique used by the Erudite when creating their serums.

But given the complexity of the serums in the Divergent series—they must target a wide variety of different neuronal networks and individual neurons, they must simultaneously stifle neurotransmitters while firing others, and so forth—it can't be simple to create the nano-serum.

In the real world, when scientists have a complex drug with many active ingredients, they might someday use a process called nanoprecipitation to deliver the particles. A brief explanation of this research process is that a large amount of the drug is dissolved in a solvent, and then the supersaturated solution is added to an anti-solvent. This technique produces nanocrystals of the drug.

Brain-specific nanoparticle research is in its infancy, so as I've pointed out in this book already, what we see in *Divergent* is far-future technology. One reason is that not enough is known about brain diseases that might be treated with nanoparticle drugs. Also, it remains difficult to devise formulations that can target and deliver nano-drugs to specific areas of the brain.

The Pharmaceutical Research and Manufacturers of America reports that institutions and companies are working on 444 types of medicines that target the brain.[8] However, none of these drugs force us to move in specific ways, make us see things that aren't there, hear sounds that don't exist, simulate terrifying environments, and so forth. Instead, these brain-specific medicines are related to potential solutions for diseases such as multiple sclerosis, Parkinson's, brain tumors, chronic pain, Alzheimer's, and epilepsy, among others.[9]

Some examples of brain-specific medical nanoparticles that are currently in the research phase are listed below. These nanoparticle drugs affect the brain in ways that would be useful to the Erudite in creating the *Divergent* serums.

- Capric glyceride nanoemulsion called Clobazam used to treat epileptic seizures
- Olanzapine used to treat schizophrenia and bipolar disorder
- Sulpiride used to treat schizophrenia

as well as a variety of nanoparticle drugs that may alleviate pain and provide therapy for Parkinson's disease, Alzheimer's disease, convulsions, AIDS, and cancer.

As with the *Divergent* simulations that take place in enclosed, controlled rooms, is it possible for electrodes to enable somebody to measure what a person is thinking and what choices she is making, all while she is hallucinating? We'll find out in a second.

The simulations also take place outside enclosed controlled rooms, where electrodes aren't going to cut it. For example, after Tris passes her final evaluation, Eric shoots an orange-brown liquid into her neck. Apparently, this serum contains long-range transmitters that wire a person's brain into the simulation programs.

Can a microscopic transmitter send neurotransmission information to a distant computer? Can that computer transmit info into the person's brain? Is it possible for both Tris and

Tobias (Four) to be in the same simulation at the same time, and to interact with each other in that simulation?

Let's try to puzzle through how we measure a person's brain activity in the real world and see if it makes sense in the futuristic *Divergent* scenario. We'll alo delve into how the nano-transmitters, or nanobots, might work.

Researchers today use physiological measurements via electrodes, helmets, goggles, and gloves to track what's happening to a user in a virtual reality immersion. Remember that our muscles, skin, blood vessels, and joints send sensory input to the brain. The body uses these inputs to regulate our heart and respiratory rates, body temperatures, blood pressure, and reflexes. By tracking and analyzing all this data, virtual reality immersion software can help researchers determine whether a person is scared, excited, looking around three-dimensional corners, deciding to take one fork in the virtual game rather than another, and so forth. However, in the virtual reality immersion scenario just described, the electrodes and other equipment aren't recording, analyzing, and revising the neurotransmitter events in the brain's receptor sites.

Scientists studying the brain employ techniques that go well beyond the mechanisms used by virtual reality researchers. Modern technology enables neuroscientists to use lights and sounds, among other things, and then watch a person's brain waves fluctuate in response to these stimuli. However, we still don't know how these brain waves relate to the person's awareness of what has happened, his feelings in response to the stimuli, or his perception of pain, anxiety, stress, happiness, and so forth.

It all boils down to electrical signals inside our bodies and brains, the movements of ions, the neurotransmissions.

If anything breaks down in this "electrical" system, our

physical, emotional, and mental health could be at risk. For example, if the eye's rod and cone photoreceptors cease to translate light into the signals needed by the brain for vision, then a person goes blind. If the hair cells within the inner ear's cochlea die, then the ear cannot process incoming sound waves, and the person goes deaf. If the spinal cord's nerve cells are damaged, then they might not be able to transmit signals from the brain's motor cortex to the legs and feet muscles, causing paralysis. In addition, the person might not process information from his skin correctly. If he touches fire or other dangerous substances, his body might not be able to transfer signals from the skin to the brain's somatosensory system.

Because the above examples (and others) are so catastrophic, scientists have been working for years to figure out ways to reverse these types of damages to the nervous system. How? You'll be fascinated to learn that, just as the *Divergent* world uses nano-circuitry to transmit signals to and from the brain, real world technology uses extremely tiny integrated electronic components to offer neural prosthetics to patients. These aren't quite nano-sized, of course—not yet, anyway— but they are remarkable, all the same. For example, doctors can implant these tiny electronics into our eyes, our muscles, our ears, and yes, even into our brains. Just as in the *Divergent* world, modern neural prosthetics interact directly with the nervous system. They supply signals to the nerves and muscles. And they also *record* signals from the nerves and muscles. This is how a paralyzed person, for example, can turn on a television or use an ordinary computer. A neural device—we'll call it a "transmitter" to conform to *Divergent* terminology—can obtain and then transmit electrical signals from a person's nervous system in order to switch on the tube or operate the computer.

It's not as simple as slipping on an armband or a cap. It requires surgical implantation of the neural device.

It was exciting back in 2006 when a study published in *Nature* magazine provided the first results from such a system.[10] In this study, scientists led by John Donoghue of Brown University surgically implanted neural devices in a paralyzed patient. The transmissions from the patient's mind enabled him to move a computer cursor, send e-mail, switch channels on a television, and make a robotic arm pick up some candy and drop it into somebody else's hand. Surgeons placed a silicon chip containing one hundred electrodes into the man's brain. These electrodes fed information to a computer interface that recorded the neurotransmissions from hundreds of the brain's motor cortex neurons.

Just as in *Divergent,* the scientists recorded signals from an individual's brain, and in the real-world case, used those signals to help somebody who previously had no hope to overcome his disability. The motivations of the Erudite aren't quite so pure, to put it mildly.

In 2012, a device called the iBrain made headlines when the famous physicist, Stephen Hawking, used it to communicate his thoughts. The iBrain, which does not require surgical implantation, sat on Hawking in the form of a head band. Neuroscientist Philip Low, who devised the algorithm used by the device to interpret brain signals, explained that the idea behind the iBrain experiment with Hawking was to see if he "can use his mind to create a consistent and repeatable pattern that a computer can translate into, say, a word or letter or a command for a computer."[11] As Hawking thought about making a fist with his right hand, the computer displayed a change in the spikes representing the brain's signals.

The first neural prosthetic, the cochlear implant, was first used in the early 1970s. These advanced hearing aids enable once-deaf people to have conversations with others. Because the hearing devices were so successful, with tens of thousands of people helped by them, scientists started working on eye implants, which contain electrodes that sit directly on the retina. These electrodes perform the functions of a blind person's damaged rod and cone light receptors.

Similar to how the "transmitters" might pick up signals in *Divergent,* today's neural implants for vision and hearing work directly inside the brain. Some patients with neural prostheses in their eyes or ears still cannot see or hear sounds. This is because the nerves extending from their eyes or ears are so damaged that they cannot transport signals. Hence, the newer technologies must circumvent the use of the actual eyes or ears, and must deal directly with the visual and auditory parts of the brain.

The neural prosthetics just described would not suffice when the Erudite turn the Dauntless traitors into shuffling zombified killers. Instead, another method would be required to make the Dauntless traitors walk in rhythm with each other. This is not the same thing as a paralyzed patient lifting a robotic arm or switching a television channel. In the Dauntless case, the transmissions command the legs and arms of the person's body to move. However, other methods *could* be used by the Erudite based on modern technology and where it's heading.

Quadriplegics are paralyzed from their necks down. Using a technique called functional electrical stimulation, scientists implant electrodes directly into the muscles of quadriplegics, enabling them to stand and very slowly take a step. Jolts of electricity activate the electrodes, which then make the muscles move.

On September 26, 2013, newspapers were abuzz with reports about a man who can now control his prosthetic leg and foot simply by thinking, hence enabling him to walk and climb stairs. He's the first person who has been able to do this. According to *The Wall Street Journal,* "Aided by sensors receiving impulses from nerves and muscles that once carried signals to his missing knee and ankle, the patient was able to climb and descend stairs and walk up and down inclines much as he would with a natural leg, based on directions that came from his brain."[12] The patient in question, Zac Vawter, was in a motorcycle accident that cost him his right leg.

The method used sounds like functional electrical stimulation. In the scientific paper about the new "bionic" device,[13] the research team led by Dr. Levi J. Hargrove of the Center for Bionic Medicine, Rehabilitation Institute of Chicago, explains that right after Zac Vawter's accident, doctors implanted nerves in the hamstring muscles of his right thigh. Some of these nerves relay signals from his brain to the right ankle. So when Vawter is thinking that he wants to take a step, for example, his brain sends signals down these nerves to the right hamstring muscles. Implanted electrodes pick up these signals, which are then decoded by software algorithms that translate them into signals for actual prosthetic movements.

Says Melissa Healy of the *Los Angeles Times,* "If he wants his artificial toes to curl toward him, or his artificial ankle to shift so he can walk down a ramp, all he has to do is imagine such movements."[14]

But the device, cool as it is, still doesn't approach what we see in *Divergent.* For the real-world mechanism to control movements via brain control requires a complex and sophisticated piece of machinery. The prosthetic device is made of aluminum, has two independent motors, includes a gyroscope and an accelerometer, and weighs more than ten pounds. This is a far cry from the injection of serums and transmitters that enable the Erudite to control the movements of an army of Divergents.

Research in the real world is also moving forward to create a neural prosthetic system that incorporates touch. This type of system inputs and then transmits the touch receptor signals in a paralyzed hand directly to the neural prosthesis device. The device has software that analyzes the pressure on the skin and provides the appropriate stimulation to the hand. Eventually, scientists hope to input and then transmit the touch receptor signals directly into the brain's somatosensory cortex, which would make the system seem a lot more like the movement serums in Divergent.

Of extreme interest when considering how the *Divergent* science works is the fact that scientists also hope to surgically implant electrodes in the brain's motor cortex, then record the person's *intentions to move*. Then this neural system would activate the functional electrical stimulation implants. In other words, as with the Hawking experiment, a paralyzed person would need only think that he wants to move in a particular way, and the neural prosthetic system would take care of the rest.

This could be done with the *Divergent* movement serums. The signals in the motor cortex that initiate the movement of a leg, for example, are action potentials that occur in the motor cortex. Tiny nano-scaled devices, the nanobots, could trigger these action potentials and hence make the person move his leg.

This is all theoretical, of course. I'm giving you my ideas as to how the *Divergent* science might work based on what I know about current technology.

SERUMS AND TRANSMITTERS VERSUS PROSTHESES

In some ways, the *Divergent* method of controlling a person's sensory organs—what she hears, sees, touches, and so forth—is superior to the method used by neural prostheses.

In the human body, charged particles called ions flow through out tissue. This flow can be considered a type of electrical current, albeit a biological one.

In an electrode or neural device, the flow of electricity differs from the natural flow inside our bodies. In the conducting metal of an electrode, electricity is in the form of electrons rather than ions.

This is a very important distinction when thinking about nanobot delivery of drugs, or serums, versus the use of an actual device to record and revise what happens in the brain.

So what happens at the interface of an electrode with our body tissue? The flow of electricity becomes ionic at that intersection. Sodium and chloride ions, as discussed earlier in this book, are central to how neurotransmitters work. Hence, our body tissue contains salt water. But salt on metal creates rust, and so the metal electrode begins to corrode, making the situation dangerous and unhealthy. This does not happen with the nanobot-serum method.

But even if we someday implant electrodes directly into the brain, which again is still far less futuristic than the *Divergent* technologies, all sorts of additional complications will require resolutions. For example, let's just look at the electrode itself.

With today's technology, electrodes already come in many shapes and sizes, and they have many diverse functions. Doctors implant them in the ears, eyes, muscles, and brains of patients. Electrodes on the brain's surface might be flat, while other electrodes penetrate the brain via a large number of tiny pins. In some ear implants, coils containing tiny electrodes wind through the cochlea, yet other methods of supplying sound use auditory implants that penetrate the brainstem. Some electrodes are tiny enough to be injected into muscles, while others are long enough to go through the spinal discs that sit on muscles and then poke into the muscles themselves.

There may be risks and problems associated with the materials used for electrodes, as well. I already mentioned that salt from the human body on an electrode metal may create rust, causing corrosion of the electrode. But there are other issues.

When electrodes are stimulated, they create by-products based on their composition. So for example, silver, which was used in early neural prosthetics, creates a high amount of toxicity in the brain. So does copper. Pioneering research into neural prosthetics suggested that the electrodes be made from metals such as platinum or iridium. Complicating matters, the scientists suggested that doctors inject certain positive and negative charges and use particular pulse rates and amplitudes. In addition, when we implant something in the brain, our bodies create scar tissue around the object. This is also true when we introduce other foreign objects into our bodies.

Even platinum and iridium electrodes are affected by these and many other parameters. While these metals might suffice for surface electrodes, they don't work well in sharp-pointed electrodes that penetrate tissue and muscle. Think about it. A surface electrode might be flat and deliver electrical current to a wider surface. A sharp-pointed electrode delivers current in a concentrated dose. So with a concentrated dose of current blasting from the sharp-pointed electrode, *what happens*?

Well, the ions start piling up in the tissue by the electrode, and simultaneously, the electrons start piling up in the point of the electrode. The intersection of electrode with tissue becomes a toxic place with too much charge.

An electron, the form of current in metal, is quite different from an ion, the form of current in our bodies. For one thing, the ion is an atom that has gained or lost an electron, thus giving the atom a charge. The atom, remember, has a nucleus with electrically positive protons surrounded by negatively charged electrons. When the electrons in the metal blast from the point of an electrode, they cannot flow through the human tissue. In addition, the ions near the device cannot flow from the human tissue into the tip of the electrode.

Eventually, the electrons neutralize ions, and hence, the current flows from the electrode into the tissue. However, the metal has corroded, even if platinum and iridium alloys are used. The corrosion introduces toxic substances into the human body.

It's possible to use iridium coated with iridium oxide for the electrode. This may help the current to flow from the tip of the electrode into the body before the metal corrodes. A team of scientists from a variety of laboratories demonstrated that this technique worked but that these tiny implantable micro-electrodes still had "several shortcomings, including: high material cost, labor-intensive processing, and deterioration of long term stability."[15] The 1987 patent for neural electrodes coated in iridium oxide is held by Lois S. Robblee.[16]

So let's say that somehow scientists are able to devise a metal that is suitable, long-lasting, and safe for neural microelectrodes. As you might have guessed, there are even more problems to consider.

Does it suffice to have a sharp-pointed electrode jabbed

into the brain? Well, not really. The brain has an extremely dense amount of blood vessels, meaning that when something jabs into it, the brain bleeds—quickly and profusely. So any electrode designed to control our neurotransmissions must be shaped to avoid this dense thickets of blood vessels.

Shooting and injecting transmitters into the people of the *Divergent* world could break this mesh of blood vessels and cause internal bleeding and death. You might suppose that the transmitters—and their "electrode-type" mechanisms—must be nanoscopic to avoid the dense mesh, but remember, if the electrodes themselves are too small, the concentration of current becomes too high and toxicity occurs.

The penetrating electrode auditory brain stem implant, or PABI, is a form of the technology that penetrates the brain stem to aid in hearing and contains eight electrodes of varying lengths. For the visual neural implant, the corresponding device contains at least a thousand electrodes. Imagine what could happen to the brain should a transmitter be injected that contains more than a thousand electrodes!

As advanced as the PABI device for hearing is, it sadly doesn't work as well as we might hope. In 2008, researchers reported that "less than 25% of penetrating electrodes resulted in auditory sensations, whereas more than 60% of surface electrodes were effective. Even after more than 3 years of experience, patients using penetrating electrodes did not achieve improved speech recognition compared with those using surface electrode ABIs."[17]

Technology is clearly shifting toward smaller and smaller components. One of the latest neural prosthesis technologies uses what is called beam lead technology, in which integrated circuits are made out of silicon chips with gold leads that connect to other electronics. For the neural prosthesis, it is hoped that the tiny gold leads on the implantable devices will act as electrodes that pick up neurotransmissions. While silicon wafers have become increasingly miniaturized for placement into the brain, this means they have become more easily prone to breakage inside the tissue.

Scientists are also working to create a neural implant that not only has electrodes but also delivers drugs. If an implanted device detects certain neural activity, it can either stimulate the brain using electrodes or it can release medications. To do the latter might require a reservoir of drugs located near the skin's surface so doctors can replenish the drug supply. You could think of this futuristic technique as a precursor of the *Divergent* technology that uses transmitters (computers) and serums (drugs).

I don't want to delve *too far* into the detailed science in this book, so suffice it to say that anything we implant or inject into our brains of a prosthetic nature must be carefully devised and applied with extremely cautious measurements and techniques. Simply injecting serums and transmitters in the real world would be highly risky. The metals used to create the transmitters in *Divergent* must be exceedingly sophisticated. The shapes of the "electrodes" in the transmitter devices must be precise. If the devices are transmitting information to and from the brain, then they must have an electrode-type of capability, and they must be formed out of some type of material. All extremely complex, but not so complex as some final wrinkles in the *Divergent* puzzle.

I'm not quite sure how Tris and Tobias (Four) can interact in the same simulation at the same time. This might require that neural transmissions are received— rapidly, and in fact, I'd go so far as to suggest as rapidly as our brain *thinks*—by a computer and analyzed, and then different sets of neural transmissions are sent by that computer—again, all of this happening as quickly as our brain thinks—to both individuals.

I'm also not quite sure how Tris can fight the serums and simulations. If they are as sophisticated as what I've described in this chapter, then how does her neural circuitry literally overcome the forced stimulation of neurotransmissions?

One thing that is clear is that it wouldn't be particularly hard to induce fear in people in the *Divergent* world. Which is the subject of the next chapter, so read on. . . .

INDUCING FEAR
AND ERASING
MEMORIES

Fear plays a big part in the Divergent series, with simulations constructed specifically to play upon peoples' worst fears. In fact, we're told that the fear serum stimulates the amygdala and induces hallucinations based on the a person's fears. But Will later explains that it's the thalamus that induces fear. So what is the amygdala, what's the thalamus, and how do our bodies produce and handle fear? In fact, just what is fear?

In *Divergent*, the Dauntless leaders and the Erudite use fear as a weapon. The people allow the leaders and the Erudite to manipulate them in this way. While trying to escape their own fears, Tris and the Dauntless seem to fall increasingly under the power of those fears. They don't really escape their fears; instead, they turn inward, let the fears crystallize and harden them, and their personalities change as a result of the fears. In other words, escaping their fears doesn't make them more free to do as they wish; it makes them much less free and much more confined to a way of life they couldn't have imagined before starting the initiation process.

The people in the world of *Divergent* are conditioned by fear. They live isolated from one another in factions out of fear that any contact with other ways of thinking will cause war, torture, death. Their fears have been distorted over time into grotesque, looming horrors, and so they stay semi-content in their isolated factions, telling themselves that it's all for the best. It is fear that drives their entire society.

Fear is often disguised as courage. In the real world, teen drivers are notorious for speeding and taking more risks than their more stodgy, older counterparts. Three boys in a car with one driving and his two friends egging him on: drive faster, beat that other guy and make him feel like a loser. This is the classic stuff of a lot of teen movies, and we've all seen the classic scenes in which the stoplight goes from red to green, and *blam,* the two cars zoom off with a bunch of guys hooting. The teen driver isn't displaying bravery, *not really,* in this classic case. In fact, it's just the opposite. He's afraid of being viewed as a sissy. His fear of how others will perceive him is much bigger than his fear of injury. He won't acknowledge his fear; he won't suggest to his friends that they not speed and out-race the other car.

In the world of *Divergent,* fear is also disguised as courage when the Dauntless leap off speeding trains and skyscrapers. The Dauntless teen's fear of how others will perceive him is much bigger than his fear of injury. He won't acknowledge his fear; he won't suggest to the other Dauntless initiates that they not leap off speeding trains and skyscrapers.

Fear comes in other disguises, too, such as self-sacrifice, humility, missionary zeal, extreme respectability, fake bohemianism, bigotry and prejudice, the need to be the life of the party, the need to be a wallflower, loyalty, ambition, self-indulgence, materialism, having a chip on the shoulder and claiming everyone else is stupid or wrong, self-pity, chauvinism, and more.

Let's look at a few examples, the first one being the last on my above list: chauvinism. What is a man afraid of when he treats women as if they are inferior to men? He's afraid that he will be seen as less powerful, less potent, less important. The man is afraid of being viewed a certain way. It's his fear that drives him to become a chauvinist pig.

Or what about fake bohemianism? This typically refers to a person who displays the pretenses she thinks are associated with creative individuals. In other words, she thinks that by dressing a certain "artsy" way, by putting on particular airs, by acting as if she is an artist of some kind (or a writer, poet, musician, dancer, etc.), she will somehow project the image upon other people that she is indeed the real deal; but she isn't, and in her heart, she knows that this is the case. She's *afraid* of being viewed as somebody who is not creative and "artsy." She's afraid that people won't view her as liberal and freethinking and "cool" and somehow elevated above them.

The person who needs to be the life of the party may very well lack self-confidence. She needs to feel as if she's the most beautiful girl in the room. She needs to feel as if she's the most popular, the most important. If she had more confidence in herself, she wouldn't be this needy for other people's approval and flattery. If a person fails to flatter her enough, she has no interest in him. She is afraid of being viewed as a wallflower, a loser, as someone who might not be all that attractive, and so forth. Fear drives her actions and how she treats other people.

People are afraid to see themselves as they really are: frightened, lacking self-confidence, lacking true creativity, having sensitivity, and so on. What they perceive as their own faults become magnified in their minds, and hence, they might project personas quite opposite to reality.

Fear is often defined as what we feel when we think we are endangered in some way. We focus on self-defense, we either fight or we flee—commonly called fight or flight.

Fear springing from real threats, such as intruders with guns or bombs being dropped or rabid animals attacking us, results in survival instincts. In this manner, fear has always been critical to the continuation of the human race.

Unfortunately, many fears don't spring from real threats. Instead, they spring from perceived threats, such as all the ones—and more—that I mentioned in previous paragraphs. In this manner, fear can be self-defeating rather than helping us survive. Without a need for self-defense, a person operates out of perceived fear and raises all sorts of unnecessary and bizarre self-defenses. This type of fear makes people withdraw from situations that might be in their own self-interest. This type of fear makes people reject those who could be their closest friends and allies if only given half a chance.

In *Divergent,* society is driven by fear disguised as strength, fear disguised as love, and fear disguised as goodness. When individuals in *Divergent* simulate strengths such as selflessness, kindness, honesty, bravery, and intelligence, they may not completely feel these attributes in themselves. The selfless

Abnegation may also feel in her heart, as does Tris, that she also is brave and intelligent. The smart Erudite may feel kindness or bravery. The honest Candor may recognize kindness and selflessness in his true innermost feelings. Everyone is submerging personality attributes in order to pretend, or simulate, that they possess their faction's strengths. When they misbehave, as do the Erudite, they pretend it's for the common good. All these fears exploit everybody else in the society because each person is using everyone else to make himself feel okay and to achieve his personal goals—in short, to use other people as a means to his own ends.

It is possible, as in the *Divergent* simulations, to measure the body's reaction to fear. It's true that when a person is afraid, her heart rate accelerates and sends blood pumping through her veins, hence increasing her blood pressure. This is her body's way of ensuring that her muscles have sufficient oxygen to fight or flee. In addition, when someone is in a high-stress or terrifying situation, his body shuts down various systems that aren't critical to the fight-or-flight response. For example, the digestive system produces less saliva, which is why the frightened person's mouth might become dry. In case the body is injured during flight, the blood vessels near the skin tighten, which might help reduce bleeding. The pupils in a frightened person's eyes dilate so she can focus on movements and protect herself quickly. And of course, we all know that when we're scared, the tiny hairs on our arms prick and stand up, which could help the body sense movements and again, protect itself more quickly.

So it is indeed true that someone running a simulation can monitor Tris's vital signs and know that she has been able to slow the racing of her heart. It's also true that by stimulating the amygdala, a person running a simulation on somebody else could cause the other person to become terrified.

Beneath the temporal lobe in each half of the brain is the almond-shaped cluster of neurons called the amygdala. If the amygdala is damaged, a person may become fearless. This has been shown when people accidentally suffer brain injuries that damage the amydala or when researchers damage the brains of monkeys. When fearless, the victim of injury (or experimental destruction of his amgydala) will exhibit increased social and sexual behaviors. They will also disassociate what they see and recognize from how they feel. So a monkey, for example, may not fear something in the lab that he usually is terrified of; instead, he will get close to the object, reach past it, even touch it.

In 1923, French psychiatrist Joseph Capgras identified a syndrome after he'd been working for a decade with a female patient who thought her own husband and children were duplicate impostors. When somebody is suffering from what is now known as Capgras syndrome, he may think that impostors of some kind have replaced his loved ones. This is a rare illness, in which connections are damaged between the amygdala and the cortex in the temporal lobe. The cortex enables us to recognize faces, so while someone with Capgras syndrome may "sort of" recognize his mother, his cortex and amygdala aren't in sync, not enabling him to truly recognize her and respond appropriately. It's as if the woman *looks* like his mother. It's as if he's living in the 1956 film, *Invasion of the Body Snatchers,* in which replica impostors—in this case, aliens—have replaced everybody he knows.

Capgras occurs because the amygdala is part of the limbic system, which integrates our emotions with memories and instills fear in us. This is why the amygdala is so important when we have to cope with fear. If a raging beast attacks us in the wilderness, we remember that this is not a good thing and that we should be afraid.

In recent years, serums and other potions that stimulate the amygdala to produce fear have become popular devices in our fiction. For example, in Suzanne Collins's *Mockingjay*, tracker jacker venom is said to hijack somebody's brain by targeting the part of the brain that controls fear. Peeta, when injected with the tracker jacker venom, does not remember what is real and what is not real. His memories become distorted, or hijacked, by the venom. His brain stores fake memories instead of real ones.

Is it also true, as stated in *Divergent*, that the thalamus produces fear, or is it just the amygdala? *Divergent* gets it right on both counts.

If somebody is frightened, her amygdala sends signals to her hypothalamus, which then stimulates the pituitary gland. The hypothalamus basically connects the nervous system to the endocrine system via the pituitary gland. Under control of the hypothalamus, the pituitary releases hormones that regulate a wide variety of body functions, including growth, hunger, thirst, and also release of adrenaline from the adrenal glands.

After receiving the amygdala's "fear" signals, the hypothalamus activates the sympathetic nervous system, which then triggers the sympatho-adrenal response, "fight or flight." Both adrenaline and acetylcholine are secreted, and the person's heartbeat increases, her pupils dilate, she sweats, her mouth goes dry, and so on.

To give the frightened person better reflexes, the amygdala also transmits signals to the reticular nucleus. To enable the person's face to show fear, the amygdala sends impulses to the nuclei of the facial and trigeminal nerves.

The frightened person receives acute sensory data from her ears, eyes, skin, and so on, and this information enters her amygdala, where it is associated with specific sensory stimuli received in the past when she was frightened. When she was young and running from a bully, her heart raced, the hairs on her skin rose, her breathing accelerated, and so forth, and these memories are associated with fear of the kind she feels now.

The association between fear and the sensory stimuli may be due to the potential of the involved neuronal synapses to react quickly.

Synaptic plasticity is a term that loosely references what happens when neuronal synapses are strengthened and reinforced over time. This prolonged and repeated enhancement of synaptic efficiency is critical to our abilities to learn and remember things.

If Tris is afraid of drowning, when she's in a simulation that is "drowning" her, the amygdala remembers the horrifying experience from her past and releases two hormones, adrenaline, aka epinephrine and norepinephinre, into her bloodstream. These hormones make her heart race and supply blood to her muscles.

Approximately a decade ago, scientists discovered that the GRP and stathmin genes, both expressed in the lateral nucleus of the amygdala, can contribute to the lack of fear in animals. Mice lacking these genes become more bold and aggressive. It's possible that in the future, these genes could be used to inhibit somebody's amygdala from learning how to be afraid of things.

Much of this work was done by Nobel Prize–winner professor Eric R. Kandel of Columbia University, whose overall research may help us understand why some individuals—we can think of them as the Divergent—can remain relaxed during crises and intensely stressful situations. A 2008 research summary by the Howard Hughes Medical Institute explains that Kandel and Daniela D. Pollak were able to inhibit fear in mice so the animals felt relaxed and safe in what ordinarily would be stressful environments. The summary quotes Kandel as saying that the "behavioral changes observed in the mice squelched anxiety as effectively as antidepressant drugs such as Prozac."[1]

What are your worst fears? Do you think it's as simple as twiddling with a couple of genes and proteins in your body to get rid of those fears? Or would it take something more?

How would you rank these fears in order of terror?

- Drowning.
- Burning to death.
- Slowly suffocating.
- Losing your mind.
- Being unable to save your own child from pain or death.
- Being unable to save your own mother from pain or death.

For me, the worst fears involve harm or death to my loved ones. This is probably true for most people. Which isn't to say that other fears aren't so creepy that I would let my conscious mind think about them. Worrying about these sorts of things is akin to worrying about a nuclear holocaust.

Tris's worst fear is having to choose between her own death or shooting her family. Her second worst fear is watching her family slowly bleed to death and not being able to save them. Which isn't to say that her other fears don't terrify her, for they do.

If Professor Kandel and his associates have indeed found a mechanism that someday helps humans overcome our fears, do you think it will work to overcome a fear as significant as those involving harm and death to loved ones? I would hate to think that we can get past this type of fear. If our future technology enables us to stifle internal fears, even these truly horrific ones, will we still be human? Or will we all become heartless and uncaring? At a different level, if we're unafraid of natural dangers, our survival will be at risk, and the human race could become extinct.

The same is true if we're able to erase our memories. If we don't remember our family members and best friends, we might not take extra care to protect them and be kind toward them. By erasing our memories, wouldn't we be erasing *who we are*? A complete erasure would make us imbeciles, so as the case in *Allegiant*, only a partial and very selective erasure would make any sense at all.

As mentioned, Veronica Roth's selective memory erasure reminds me of Peeta's tracker jacker venom in *The Hunger Games*. It also reminds me of modern research aimed at doing this very thing: erasing our memories. In the not-so-distant future, scientists will be able to delete "single, specific memories while leaving other memories intact."[2] In research labs, scientists are already injecting what they term an "amnesia drug" into a test subject *while he is remembering something specific*. The amnesia drug alters the test subject's memory and, in some cases, totally erases it.

McGill University Professor Karim Nader, who performs research into amnesia drugs explains that memories from a person's past are in long-term storage in his brain. When he remembers something from long ago, he pluck those memories from his long-term storage. When he's done thinking about long ago, his brain sticks the memories back in storage, and at this point, if he's given the amnesia drug, his brain may fail to store the memories again. Hence, the drug erases the memories.[3]

A similar thing happens when we form a new memory. Principal Director of the Center for the Neuroscience of Fear and Anxiety, Professor Joseph LeDoux explains the process: "Each time you form a memory, your brain begins to form that memory in a temporary way that can be interfered with if nothing else happens. So you have to convert a temporary memory into a longterm memory in order to have that memory at some time in the future . . . instead of giving the protein synthesis inhibitor after learning and blocking consolidation, you give it after the retrieval of a previously consolidated memory. . . ."[4]

Of course, in *Allegiant,* the plan is to spread a memory-erasure serum throughout the population. The serum will operate like a virus and infect people just like a flu. If the memory-erasing serum works as in real life, then it would have to be administered before a person stores his memories. If instead the memory-erasing serum spreads like a virus, then it seems improbable that it can erase specific memories and leave others intact. Matthew in *Allegiant* does admit that the serum will erase important memories, but he adds that people can "relearn" these important memories later. I would argue that wholesale erasure of memories is unwise and that it's not possible to relearn many of our memories once they're lost. For example, I'm a writer. If a memory serum virus hits me and cuts a wide swath through my brain, erasing most of my memories, how will I ever learn how to write again the way I write now? It wouldn't be possible. What I do now, I could not do twenty years ago. My writing style in fiction has changed over the years; it has matured and evolved. There's no way I can relearn a twenty-year process!

Regardless, whether we're talking about fear, memories, intelligence, or other traits, by suppressing or changing who we are, don't we lose the essence of individuality, the potential for scientific discoveries, creativity, and everything else that makes us human? David, the leader of the Bureau of Genetic Welfare in *Allegiant,* makes this point when he's telling Tris about how his people have been "editing humanity" with genetic-manipulation experiments.

8

GADGETS AND GIZMOS

In addition to neural manipulations, serums, simulations, and micro- or nano-computer transmissions, the Divergent series mentions a few other futuristic technologies. These are touched upon almost in passing but are worth noting here for the sake of completion.

At one point, Caleb mentions water-filtration systems, and Tobias adds that the Amity use "aquaponics" as one method to grow food. A bit later, we're told that the Erudite developed a "better than dirt" mineral solution for growing plants that increases the rate of new-cell production.

A MINI-LOOK AT FOUR

Tobias Eaton has four fears, hence his Dauntless nickname of Four. He and Tris fall in love, as they have much in common in this torn and difficult world. For one thing, both Four and Tris were born into the Abnegation faction and then chose Dauntless at their Choosing Ceremonies. For another, both of them appear to be Divergent—Tris actually is Divergent, and Four displays many key Divergent-like attributes. But most important, both Four and Tris display empathy for others, a keen intelligence that enables them to survive in the Dauntless world while taking care of other people, and an ability to stifle their fears, probably Tris more than Four. In fact, we know that Four has feelings for Tris when, despite his fear of heights, he tries to climb a Ferris wheel to make sure she's okay.

Four has a bizarre family life. His mother, Evelyn Johnson-Eaton, pretended to be dead, when in reality she left his father and is the leader of the Factionless. She could be considered a good person for documenting the number of Divergent within the Factionless and for trying to help the Factionless usurp the authority and destroy the power of the Erudite. Or as Four has always thought, she could be considered a bad person for leaving Four in the hands of Marcus, and as Tris constantly feels, she's an outright liar. Four and Tris seem to be correct because, as the old saying goes, "absolute power corrupts absolutely," and it does turn out that after the Factionless assume some power, Evelyn says that everyone who resisted her efforts will be punished.

Evelyn explains that she thought Four would be safer with Marcus than with her because Marcus told her that their son might very well be Divergent. I'm not exactly sure why this logic holds true. If Evelyn is a good person, who wants the Factionless and Divergent to establish a fair and reasonable new society that helps everybody, then why does it matter if her son, Tobias, is a Divergent? It might make more sense to enlist his help as he's growing up, because after all, he ends up being a Dauntless leader as a teenager, and being Dauntless isn't exactly a safe way of living. There's no way she could have guessed when he was just a kid that he would grow up to join Dauntless and then want to become a leader to help the Dauntless ally with the Factionless. And given that she decides to punish people who didn't support her efforts to take over and crush the factions, we know she doesn't have everybody's best interests at heart. So she's probably lying when she tells Four that she left him with Marcus so he would be safer.

As for his father, Marcus Eaton, Four hates him and claims he was abusive and cruel when Four was growing up. In an odd twist of events, Four whips Marcus to get even for the fact that Marcus whipped Four with belts during his childhood. This odd family life makes Four a sympathetic character, particularly to Tris, who is already attracted to him.

Of course, aquaponics is used now to grow food. Such a system pumps water through a hydroponic mechanism, which uses bacteria to turn matter in the water into nitrates and nitrites that plants use for nourishment. In one part of an aquaponics system is an area with fish or other aquatic animals. Their uneaten food or debris is basically collected and processed by biofilters. In the other part of the system is where the plants grow, with their roots submerged in the nutrient-rich water. It's much more complicated than this brief description, of course, but I leave it to you to learn all about modern-day aquaponics should you be interested. It's a bit beyond the scope of this book to present a science text on such a minor topic in the Divergent series.

The one-room filtration building in *Divergent* is filled with machines that process dirty water. This is also nothing new, as we have filtration systems that pipe in dirty water, cleanse it, and re-pipe it back to our cities and towns. There's also a power plant in the *Divergent* world, which runs on wind, water, and solar energy. Somehow, this plant provides energy to the entire city, but again, this technology is nothing new, so we can easily take the brief descriptions as givens.

But what about the solar-powered cars? When Jeanine's grunts drive Tris back to the Dauntless compound, they use cars with roof panels that convert "energy into sunlight." (*Divergent*, page 361) We're not told how these cars work or why the roof panels convert energy into sunlight. I've been puzzled about this brief mention of solar-powered cars because I'd think that the panels would convert sunlight into energy rather than the other way around. But let's skip over this puzzling matter and try to determine if it's possible to fuel a car using solar energy.

The short answer is that we do indeed have solar-powered vehicles that convert sunlight into energy, but given the limitation of this form of energy, the cars are used for extremely specialized purposes.

To handle the energy conversion, this type of car uses photovoltaic, aka PV, cells typically made of silicon semiconductors. In short, when the photons in the sunlight hit the PV cells, electrons are triggered, which creates an electric current. A solar car might be able to achieve sixty miles per hour in speed and might run more than two hundred miles on their batteries.

This all sounds great, doesn't it? So if we already have solar-powered cars, why aren't they everywhere on the high-ways?

Well, for one thing, a solar-powered car may cost hundreds of thousands or even a million dollars—assuming you want to go sixty miles per hour and go for a couple hundred of miles before the battery dies. A single car may need thousands of solar cells, and the cells that convert energy efficiently and effectively may cost many hundreds of dollars each.

Another problem with solar-powered cars is an obvious one. They may not run on snowy or rainy days, and they may not run at night. The battery will eventually die.

Another technology that is briefly mentioned in these books is an earpiece with a short-range signal of only one quarter of a mile. Given that the Erudite use long-range wireless transmitters in humans, why don't they have long-range wireless earpieces? This is a minor point, but one that left me slightly curious.

Finally, a few "prototype gadgets" are mentioned, for example, by a guy named Fernando, who shows Tris and Christina a tiny metal disk that emits signals that people cannot hear. These signals, claims Fernando, could shatter all the glass windows in the Erudite headquarters building.

Another prototype is a plastic black box that Cara shows to Tris and Christina. When Cara flips a switch on the box, blue light sizzles between two metal prongs on its top. Cara says the device is a stunner.

I want to mention one final aspect of technology in this series of books. Computer technology. I'm slightly puzzled by the backups of critical Erudite data and software. Tris suggests that if they find the computers, they can simply destroy the data and software, and this will be the end of the evil simulations. Caleb, who is apparently smart enough to be an Erudite, answers that the computers can be anywhere, then Tris remembers that the control room where Tobias worked may contain the almighty computers. However, we're far into the future, given the neuroscience technology in this world. It seems unlikely that amazing backup systems would not be in place. And it seems unlikely that the Erudite would leave Tobias (of all people) in charge of an all-powerful control room. I'd think that Jeanine could easily place a "sentient" presence in the supposed control room as the computer expert rather than use Tobias. Or she could have her loyal minions monitor everything wirelessly from afar. After all, we are told that she leaves nothing to chance. Why does she bother to send soldiers back to guard these computers? This makes it sound as if we're still in the world of mainframes—circa 1960s and 1970s. Remember, the Erudite's technology is so advanced, they can control humans beings via wireless transmissions and mind-control serums and devices. Surely, they would *at least* distribute their control systems in various locations and protect everything with ample backup systems. Access to distributed computers and backup systems would require fingerprint and retina scans—again, at minimum, because these people can scan and analyze your *brain* before they provide access! Seriously, they wouldn't need to place armed guards in front of a door. Also, we're told constantly that Tobias is the most amazing computer expert around and that nobody else can do what he does. Yet to instantly stop a simulation requires only that he tap a computer screen a couple of times. Even I could do that, even you could do that; and when Tobias then rips the hard drive out of the computer, explaining that it is the only way to remove the simulation software, I have a hard time believing he's an expert. Again, there's no backup of this software and data that's stored on this little hard drive? If you hide the drive in your pocket or under your pillow, you're protecting everybody from the evil simulations? Jack does say that the Erudite did indeed back up the "footage" of the attack on the Dauntless compound all over the city. However, much later in *Insurgent,* Marcus and Cara are going to send all the Erudite data to computers in other factions. This is their attempt to "save" the data by backing it up, basically.

9

WHAT'S A UTOPIA?

In the back of the first *Divergent* novel, Veronica Roth addresses dystopian and utopian fiction. She explains that for her, a utopian novel is one in which "everything is perfect" and then goes on to tell us that *Divergent* is a utopian novel. Now, this statement may puzzle you, as it did me. The world of *Divergent* is not at all perfect. People kill each other, they sabotage each other, one faction hates another, torture is common, people have no freedom—not really—and no true way to do anything other than adhere to the rigid rules of their society. So how is this a perfect utopian world?

Ms. Roth explains that in *Divergent*, each person chooses

a "path," which I loosely interpret to mean "faction," and each person wants to be his or her very best. She briefly describes her utopian world as one in which an individual knows what's expected of him and has a clear purpose in life. For me, this doesn't exactly describe a perfect world, because I don't have much desire to adhere to arbitrary rules about my conduct, what's expected of me, and what somebody else determines my purpose in life to be. I prefer to stumble along and make these decisions on my own. You see, people *change* over the decades, and what you may think is cool for you in your teens may not line up with how you feel in your twenties, much less your later years. By choosing the wrong path early on, you could not only mess up the rest of your life, but in the case of *Divergent*, you could end up dead. Look at Al. His life isn't so perfect. He chooses Dauntless, only to find that he can't hack it. He ends up dead.

While Ms. Roth writes that Divergent "was my utopian world," she also writes that indeed her utopia is a pretty rotten place, not so perfect after all. She acknowledges what I said in the first few paragraphs of this chapter, that my ideas about a perfect world may not necessarily be the same as somebody else's. She ends up concluding that depending on how readers feel about what constitutes a perfect world, people may read the same book and while some may view it as dystopian, others may view it as utopian. What she says makes sense because it is true that if you can't think well for yourself, then having somebody else define everything for you and give you a detailed life plan might very well be a utopia. But again, I point to Al, who certainly wasn't good at choosing his life's path, and we all know how he turned out: dead.

A utopia is typically defined as a society in which everything is perfect: the society, the conditions under which people live, the laws, and the government. The term was invented in 1516 by Sir Thomas More, who wrote a book in Latin called . . . *Utopia.* Because *utopia* as a word might mean both "no place land" and "good place land," it's possible that a utopia in its literal definition is a perfect place that does not really exist. This is indeed what the original leaders of the *Divergent* world attempted to create, a perfect society where war could finally cease, but of course, this perfection does not really exist.

Global world peace is a typical model in a utopian novel. While *Divergent* doesn't suggest that the entire world is in a vapor of peace, it focuses on what might be the city of Chicago. Here, leaders long ago imposed the faction structure on the citizens in order to provide a noncombative, peaceful way of life. I suppose the thinking goes something like this: If everybody has what he or she needs and wants, then why would anybody fight? The problem is that it's innate in human nature to always want more, whether it be intellectual pursuits, exploration of ideas, creation of art or music or literature or technology, and the like. Human beings are animals, and when you get down to basics, animals are territorial and they fight over food, mates, and anything that might impede their own offspring from succeeding and reproducing. This is central to evolutionary concepts, the survival of the fittest. What society does, in general, is try to impose structures and rules upon human beings to help us control these innate impulses—for example, if you steal somebody's material possessions or take his property, you might go to jail. Without laws and structures, society would disintegrate into the Wild West, with very aggressive people of a certain nature stopping at nothing to take control of everything. It is innate to the species that there will always be people who need to control everyone and everything around them. Jeanine is a great example of this type of person. So with people like Jeanine in the world, how can we ever have global peace?

Economic parity in which capitalism no longer forces people to fight each other is another typical model in utopian fiction. In this form of fictional world, people no longer do work that they dislike. They do only what makes them happy and what also happens to serve the common good. Money no longer matters. Certainly, this is the case with *Divergent*, in which the Erudite want to use their intelligence and they do, the Abnegation want to serve the common good and they do, the Dauntless want to act as security and they do. We don't see any struggles in this world over money. In fact, we don't even know how these people get money most of the time. For example, how does Tris afford tattoos and clothes? Where does her money come from? Who pays the janitors, maids, laundresses, cooks, and other workers in the dormitories where initiates sleep, bathe, and eat? We really don't know how this society operates on a financial level.

Another type of utopian fiction portrays a society in which people live more in harmony with nature. In the United States during the 1960s, communes developed in which young people joined forces, living together, growing their own crops, sharing the food, and dividing the labor. This may have been a way of trying to return to nature and carve out a semi-utopian existence within the confines of a capitalist society. In the world of *Divergent*, the Amity live in harmony with nature and remind me of the people living on communes in the 1960s. They believe in love and peace, and they share their food with everyone else. The Abnegation are the true peaceniks because they not only believe in love and peace and sharing with other people, but they actively do all these things, as well. They help the Factionless; they serve the poor and needy and the sick. This is why the Abnegation run much of the government and make the rules. It is thought that by their very nature, the Abnegation will look out for the well-being of their fellow citizens. Of course, people being what they are, this doesn't sit well with everybody, and there are factions such as the Erudite who want more control in the overall government. As I wrote earlier, human beings are, after all, animals; many innately look out for their own interests and also the interests of their families and "tribal" groups, that is, factions.

Utopian worlds may also have advanced technologies that enable people to have better health and to live longer. Their standards of living may be enhanced as a result of scientific advances, as well. In a perfect world, would anybody suffer or die from a terrible long-term disease? The world Veronica Roth creates has some advanced technology when it comes to neuroscience and genetics, but when it comes to everything else, such as how the people live—their medical facilities, their transportation and entertainment, and so forth—this world is deplete in our current technologies, much less anything particularly futuristic.

In a perfect world, dull chores would be handled by technology, freeing people to pursue art, music, and whatever else they enjoy . . . or so goes the thinking behind this form of so-called utopian society. But you can always flip things upside down and view ideas from opposite directions, so in this case, you could argue that it's healthy for human beings to do physical labor and dull chores; it helps relieve stress, it builds muscles, it builds character.

Perhaps the original utopia was the Garden of Eden—before the snake, that is. The Bible tells us that Adam had all the food he needed, he had Eve to keep him company, and he didn't have to slave away at some dull, dead-end, horrible job. He lived in utopia, basically, until the snake came along and he munched on the apple.

If you're interested in reading utopian fiction, here are a few classic titles:

- *A Modern Utopia* (1905) by H. G. Wells. In this early novel, everyone is a vegetarian, and nobody slaughters animals and eats them anymore. In addition, women have more rights than in the real world of 1905, but they still don't have equality with the men.

- *Walden Two* (1948) by B. F. Skinner. This one is of particular interest because Skinner's novel focused on scientific ways to change the way people behave, which is similar to the fundamental idea behind *Divergent*. In *Walden Two,* there is no free will, and people's behavior is based on environmental and genetic factors. In *Divergent,* people have very little in the way of free will, and the factions they end up in and the way they therefore spend their lives is predicated in large part on genetic factors—the families and thus factions into which they are born. In *Walden Two,* people are supposed to seek ways in which to improve their rural society, and if they can prove that a change would benefit everybody, then the society allows the change. This is not the case in *Divergent*.

- *Childhood's End* (1953) by Arthur C. Clarke. In this novel, alien Overlords invade the Earth. They form a world government, end war on the planet, and eventually lead Earth into a utopian Golden Age. However, this utopia comes with a heavy price. Human innovation and creativity are stifled, and human culture suffers. Human children start displaying telepathic abilities and start merging with the cosmic intelligence known as the Overmind. They are like the Borg, just as the Dauntless traitors seem to be like the Borg—under the control of the Overmind, under the control of the Erudite. The children in Clarke's novel are no longer really "human" and live apart from their parents, who become miserable wretches.

▪ *The Left Hand of Darkness* (1969) and *The Dispossessed: An Ambiguous Utopia* (1974) by Ursula K. Le Guin. If you haven't read Ms. Le Guin's novels, you should. I suggest starting with *The Left Hand of Darkness,* which precedes and is set in the same world as *The Dispossessed.* In *The Left Hand of Darkness,* people form the League of All Worlds and the Ekumen, which governs eighty-three worlds. Genly Ai travels to a cold planet called Winter to convince its citizens to join Ekumen. On Winter, there's never been a war, and the genders are neither male nor female, which, as an aside, is a major part of this world and had a major impact on readers in 1969. In Ms. Le Guin's world, the lack of dualities, of male and female, of summer and winter, create a form of utopia.

Dystopian fiction presents societies that are so imperfect that people suffer from overall oppression, illness, and/or poverty. In dystopian novels, people struggle to survive against all sorts of horrible odds, including biological and chemical warfare, genetic engineering, global warming, pollution, plagues, government greed, and many other calamities and problems. In a postapocalyptic dystopia, something triggers the downfall of humanity, something like war or a plague. A modern classic example of postapocalyptic dystopian fiction is *The Hunger Games* series by Suzanne Collins. In her novels, Ms. Collins postulates an apocalypse followed by war and rebellion, and she pits children against each other in gladiatorial battles to the death.

Dystopian fiction has become increasingly popular in the past decade. As economies around the world falter, as wars erupt everywhere, as people find themselves out of work with their homes lost, their families hungry, and with little hope for improvement, it seems to many that life is bleak and dismal. Dystopian fiction presents life that is bleak and dismal, and hence, it underscores how many people feel these days. Dystopian fiction warns us that if we don't stop killing each other and instead start helping each other, we're all doomed. We need to change the way we behave and how we treat other before it's too late.

A classic dystopian novel is George Orwell's *1984,* in which three super-states exist after a global war. These super-states control all the citizens in their territories. Most of the citizens in the *Divergent* world have no say in their governments and their laws. In *1984,* 85 percent of the people, the proles or proletariats, also have no power and no wealth. Things are a lot worse for people in *1984,* though, because the Party keeps them impoverished and desperate for food and shelter, and it also sends out thought police to make sure people don't even think subversive things.

In *1984,* the government hides the truth and news organizations don't report reality. In the world of *Divergent,* nobody really knows what happened long ago when the factions were first formed: who did it, how did they do it, and so on?

In addition to *1984,* the 1924 novel *We* by Yevgeny Zamyatin is considered a classic example of dystopian fiction. *We* presented an oppressive government, terrorism, and complete suppression of creativity and individuality.

Ray Bradbury's *Fahrenheit 451* is another classic dystopian novel, and it also shows us how bad life might be due to brainwashing, blind faith in the government and technology, and the loss of our intellectual and individual liberties.

Brave New World by Aldous Huxley is also a classic dystopian novel, and it's similar to *Fahrenheit 451* in that it also shows readers how terrible life might be if we're all brainwashed by the government, slaves to technologies, and reduced to witless zombies who have no free will or individual liberties.

Many books combine elements of both utopia and dystopia; that is, the authors create worlds that are supposed to be perfect but possess serious flaws. I would argue that the world of *Divergent* falls into this category. While the leaders of the society have attempted to create a perfect world, what they've actually created is a world in which people do suffer, people do ignore the Factionless as impoverished losers not worthy of much help or common decency, people do fight and hurt each other and even kill each other. And in the end, everybody in the society is at war.

Rather than calling *Brave New World* a work of dystopian fiction, people often refer to it as utopian. The argument is that the characters are so brainwashed and controlled by their government that they don't really know that they're being oppressed.

This blend of dystopia and utopia is similar to what we see in *Divergent*. The oppressed people in the *Divergent* world must conform to what their factions allow them to do and think. An Abnegation cannot break into song and start dancing. An

Amity cannot join a laboratory and study genetics or computer science. A member of Dauntless cannot open a bakery and make cupcakes for a living. And yet, these people are so brainwashed and controlled by the rules and regulations of their society that most of them don't even realize they're being oppressed.

REFERENCES

Chapter 1. What's in This Book?

1. Karen Springen, "E-Stories for 'Divergent' Fans Awaiting 'Allegiant,'" *Publishers Weekly*, June 20, 2013, www.pub lishersweekly.com/pw/by-topic/childrens/childrens-book -news/article/57904-e-stories-for-divergent-fans-awaiting -allegiant.html.

Chapter 2. Factions and Free Will

1. Veronica Roth, *Divergent*, (New York: HarperCollins, 2011), "Bonus Materials" in the back of the book, p. 8.
2. Renuka Bhaskar, Belkinés Arenas-Germosén, and

Christopher Dick, Population Division, U.S. Census Bureau, *Demographic Analysis 2010: Sensitivity Analysis of the Foreign-Born Migration Component,* May 2013, p. 5, www.census.gov/population/intmigration/.

3. Steven A. Camarota, *Immigrants in the United States, 2010: A Profile of America's Foreign-Born Population,* Center for Immigration Studies, August 2012, www.cis.org/2012-profile-of-americas-foreign-born-population.

4. U.S. Department of Commerce, United States Census Bureau, *American FactFinder,* http://factfinder2.census.gov/faces/nav/jsf/pages/community_facts.xhtml and http://factfinder2.census.gov/faces/tableservices/jsf/pages/productview.xhtml?pid=DEC_10_DP_DPDP1.

5. Ibid.

6. Veronica Roth, *Insurgent* (New York: HarperCollins, 2012), p. 523.

7. Kathleen D. Vohs and Jonathan W. Schooler, "The value of believing in free will: encouraging a belief in determinism increases cheating," *Psychological Science,* 19(1), pp. 49–54. The abstract is at: www.ncbi.nlm.nih.gov/pubmed/18181791.

Chapter 3. Neuroscience and Genetics of the Factions

1. Dr. David Whitehouse, "Genetically Altered Babies Born," BBC News Online Science Service at http://news.bbc.co.uk/2/hi/sci/tech/1312408/stm.

2. List of human genetic tests at www.fda.gov/MedicalDevices/ProductsandMedicalProcedures/InVitroDiagnostics/ucm330711.htm#human.

3. www.ncbi.nlm.nih.gov/gtr/.

4. "The Future of Genomic Medicine: Policy Implications for

Research and Medicine," National Human Genome Research Institute, National Institutes of Health, November 16, 2005, www.genome.gov/17516574.

5. Lori B. Andrews, *Future Perfect: Confronting Decisions about Genetics* (New York: Columbia University Press, 2001), pp. 10–11. Andrews is a lawyer whose credentials include advisor on genetic and reproductive technology to Congress, the World Health Organization, the National Institutes of Health, the Centers for Disease Control and Prevention, and many foreign nations.

6. Frederick B. Rudolph and Larry V. McIntire, Editors, *Biotechnology: Science, Engineering, and Ethical Challenges for the 21st Century* (Washington D.C.: Joseph Henry Press, 1996), pp. 201–202.

7. Michael G. Zey, *The Future Factor: The Five Forces Transforming Our Lives and Shaping Human Destiny* (New York: McGraw-Hill, 2000), p. 51. Zey is the executive director of the Expansionary Institute, a consultant to Fortune 500 companies and government agencies.

8. A. J. Griffith, W. Ji, M. E. Prince, R. A. Altschuler, and M. H. Meisler, "Optic, Olfactory, and Vestibular Dysmorphogenesis in the Homozygous Mouse Insertional Mutant Tg9257," *Journal of Craniofacial Genetics and Developmental Biology,* Volume 19, pp. 157–163.

9. Go to the Web site www.ornl.gov/hgmis/posters, fill in the form, and download your free *Human Genome Landmarks: Selected Traits and Disorders Mapped to Chromosomes Poster*!

Chapter 4. The Divergent and Mirror Neurons

1. Vittorio Gallese, Luciano Fadiga, Leonardo Fogassi, and Giacomo Rizzolatti, "Action Recognition in the Premotor

Cortext," *Brain,* Vol. 119, pp. 593–609 (Oxford University Press, 1996). September 2, 2013, at http://brain.oxford journals.org/content/119/2/593.full.pdf+html.

2. Giacomo Rizzolatti and Laila Craighero, "The Mirror-Neuron System," *Annual Review of Neuroscience,* Vol. 27, pp. 169–192, 2004, http://psych.colorado.edu/~kimlab/Rizzolatti.annurev.neuro.2004.pdf.

3. Temma Ehrenfeld, "Reflections on Mirror Neurons," *Association for Psychological Science Observer,* Vol. 24, No.3, March 2011, www.psychologicalscience.org/index.php/publications/observer/2011/march-11/reflections-on-mirror-neurons.html.

4. W. D. Hutchison, K. D. Davis, A. M. Lozano, R. R. Tasker, and J. O. Dostrovsky, "Pain-Related Neurons in the Human Cingulate Cortex," *Nature Neuroscience,* Vol. 2, No. 5, pp. 403–405, 1999, www.nature.com/neuro/journal/v2/n5/abs/nn0599_403.html.

5. Boris C. Bernhardt and Tania Singer, "The Neural Basis of Empathy," *Annual Review of Neuroscience,* Vol. 35, pp. 1–23, July 2012, www.annualreviews.org/doi/abs/10.1146/annurev-neuro-062111-150536.

6. Natasha Pinol, "Introspective People Have Larger Prefrontal Cortex," *Neuroscience News,* September 17, 2010, http://neurosciencenews.com/introspective-people-have-larger-prefrontal-cortex/.

7. Miranda Marquit, "New Features Found in Einstein's Brain," *PhysOrg,* April 21, 2009, http://phys.org/news159536686.html.

8. Nick Collins, "Einstein's Brain 'Exceptionally Complicated,'" *The Telegraph,* November 2012, www.telegraph.co.uk/science/science-news/9707090/Einsteins-brain-exceptionally-complicated.html.

9. Collins, Ibid.
10. Michael E. Martinez, "Everything You Know about the Brain is Wrong," *Salon,* July 21, 2013, www.salon.com/2013/07/21/everything_you_know_about_the_brain_is_wrong/.
11. Ibid.
12. F. Diane Barth, "Empathy, Understanding and Mirror Neurons," *Psychology Today,* March 2, 2013, www.psychologytoday.com/blog/the-couch/201303/empathy-understanding-and-mirror-neurons.

ADDITIONAL RESOURCES

Vittorio Gallese, "The 'Shared Manifold' Hypothesis: From Mirror Neurons to Empathy," *Journal of Consciousness Studies,* Vol. 8, No. 5–7, pp. 33–50, 2001, http://didattica.uniroma2.it/assets/uploads/corsi/33846/Gallese_2001.pdf.

Prof. Giacomo Rizzolatti will discuss the mirror mechanism and its clinical implications in the ICRAN2013, Conference Web site at http://icranconference.com/the-mirror-mechanism-a-mechanism-for-understanding-others/.

Donald W. Mackinnon, "Personality and the Realization of Creative Potential," *American Psychologist,* Vol. 20, No. 4, April 1965, pp. 273–281, http://psycnet.apa.org/journals/amp/20/4/273/,

Jun Tanji and Eiji Hoshi, "Role of the Lateral Prefrontal Cortex in Executive Behavioral Control," *Physiological Reviews,* Vol. 88, No. 1, January 2008, pp. 37–57, http://physrev.physiology.org/content/88/1/37.short.

Christopher L. Asplung, J. Jay Todd, Andy P. Snyder, and Rene Marois, "A Central Role for the Lateral Prefrontal Cortex in Goal-Directed and Stimulus-Driven Attention," *Nature Neuroscience,* Vol. 13, March 2010, pp. 507–512.

Chapter 5. Factions and the Factionless: Authoritarian Rule and Prejudices

1. T. W. Adorno, Else Frenkel-Brunswik, Daniel J. Levinson, R. Nevitt Sanford, *The Authoritarian Personality* (England: Harper & Brothers 1950). The PDF is here: www.ajcar chives.org/main.php?GroupingId=6490.
2. Ibid., p. 226.
3. www.nybooks.com/books/authors/milton-rokeach/.
4. M. Rokeach, *The Nature of Human Values* (New York: The Free Press, 1973).
5. Mike Schneider, "911 Tapes in Trayvon Martin Shooting Released," *Chicago Sun-Times*, March 17, 2012, www .suntimes.com/news/nation/11360266-418/911-tapes-in-trayvon-martin-shooting-released.html.
6. "WAOK Wants to Know:" Should George Zimmerman be Arrested for the Killing of Trayvon Martin?" *CBS Atlanta*, March 19, 2012, http://atlanta.cbslocal.com/2012/03/19 /waok-wants-to-know-should-george-zimmerman-be-ar rested-for-the-killing-of-trayvon-martin/.
7. "Transcript of George Zimmerman's Call to the Police," *Mother Jones*, www.motherjones.com/documents/326700 -full-transcript-zimmerman.
8. Lauren Effron, "George Zimmerman Could Face Civil Suits, Death Threats, Federal Prosecution," *ABC News*, July 14, 2013, http://abcnews.go.com/US/george-zim merman-face-civil-suits-death-threats-federal/story ?id=19661599.
9. "AP Poll: U.S. Majority Have Prejudice against Blacks," *USA Today*, October 27, 2012, www.usatoday.com/story /news/politics/2012/10/27/poll-black-prejudice-america /1662067/.

10. "In U.S. Religious Prejudice Stronger against Muslins," *Gallup*, January 21, 2010, www.gallup.com/poll/125312 /religious-prejudice-stronger-against-muslims.aspx.

11. *FBI Hate Crime Statistics*, 2009, www2.fbi.gov/ucr/hc2009 /victims.html.

12. *FBI Hate Crime Statistics*, 2011, www.fbi.gov/news/stories /2012/december/annual-hate-crimes-report-released/an nual-hate-crimes-report-released.

13. "Bigotry against Jews and Muslims on the Rise, Says U.S.," *BBC*, May 20, 2013, www.bbc.co.uk/news/world-us -canada-22601881.

14. "Bigotry by the Numbers," *Esquire*, May 23, 2008, www .esquire.com/features/bigotry-statistics-0608.

15. Richard H. Carmona, "50 Years Later: Prejudice Remains, but Opportunities Abound," *Huffington Post*, August 30, 2013, www.huffingtonpost.com/richard-h-carmona- md /50-years-later-prejudice-_b_3844661.html?utm_hp _ref=impact&ir=Impact.

Chapter 6. Pain-in-the-Neck Simulations and Serums

1. "The First Virtual Reality Technology to Let You See, Hear, Smell, Taste, and Touch," *PhysOrg*, March 4, 2009, http:// phys.org/news155397580.html.

2. Ray Kurzweil, "Ray Kurzweil Explores the Next Phase of Virtual Reality," *Big Think* transcript, April 27, 2009, http://bigthink.com/videos/ray-kurzweil-explores-the -next-phase-of-virtual-reality.

3. Elizabeth Millard, "Whatever Happened to Virtual Reality?" *NewsFactor Technology News*, August 30, 2002, http://technews.acm.org/articles.cfm?fo=2002-09-sep

/0904w.html with the entire article at www.newsfactor .com/perl/story/19242.html, last accessed in 2005.

4. Virginia Berridge and Griffith Edwards, *Opium and the People,* www.druglibrary.eu/library/books/opiumpeople /opiummedprac.html.

5. F. Arnold Clarkson, "Dr. John Brown of Edinburgh," Men and Books, *Canadian Medical Association Journal,* April 1952, Vol. 66, No. 4, pp. 390–395, www.ncbi.nlm.nih.gov /pmc/articles/PMC1822434/?page=1.

6. Katie Thomas, "U.S. Drug Costs Dropped in 2012, but Rises Loom," *The New York Times,* March 18, 2013, www .nytimes.com/2013/03/19/business/use-of-generics -produces-an-unusual-drop-in-drug-spending.html ?pagewanted=all&_r=0.

7. R. G. Thorne, G. J. Pronk, V. Padmanabhan, W. H. Frey II, "Delivery of insulin-like growth factor-I to the rat brain and spinal cord along olfactory and trigeminal pathways following intranasal administration," *Neuroscience,* Vol. 127, No. 2, 2004, pp. 481–496, www.ncbi.nlm.nih.gov /pubmed/15262337.

8. "Nearly 450 Innovative Medicines in Development for Neurological Disorders," Pharmaceutical Research and Manufacturers of America, www.phrma.org/press-release /innovative-medicines-in-development-for-neurological -disorders.

9. http://phrma.org/sites/default/files/pdf/MedicinesInDe velopmentNeurologicalDisorders2013.pdf.

10. "Is This the Bionic Man?" *Nature,* Vol. 442, No. 106, July 13, 2006, www.nature.com/nature/journal/v442/n7099 /full/442109a.html.

11. David Ewing Duncan, "A Little Device That's Trying to Read Your Thoughts," *The New York Times,* April 2, 2012,

www.nytimes.com/2012/04/03/science/ibrain-a-device
-that-can-read-thoughts.html?_r=0.

12. Ron Winslow, "Brain Power Enough to Control 'Bionic' Leg," *The Wall Street Journal,* September 26, 2013, p. A3.

13. Levi J. Hargrove, Ph.D.; Ann M. Simon, Ph.D.; Aaron J. Young, M.S.; Robert D. Lipschutz, C.P.; Suzanne B. Finucane, M.S.; Douglas G. Smith, M.D.; and Todd A. Kuiken, M.D., Ph.D. "Robotic Leg Control with EMG Decoding in an Amputee with Nerve Transfers," *New England Journal of Medicine,* September 26, 2013, pp. 1237–1242, http:// www.nejm.org/doi/pdf/10.1056/NEJMoa1300126.

14. Melissa Healy, "Bionic Leg Is Controlled by Brain Power," *Los Angeles Times,* September 25, 2013, www.latimes.com /science/la-sci-robotic-leg-20130926,0,7310017.story ?track=rss&utm_source=feedburner&utm_medium=feed &utm_campaign=Feed%3A+latimes%2Fnews%2Fsci ence+(L.A.+Times+-+Science).

15. Thomas S. Phely-Bobin, Thomas Tiano, Brian Farrell, Radek Fooksa, Lois Robblee, David J Edell, and Richard Czerw, "Carbon Nanotube Based Electrodes for Neuroprosthetic Applications," *Materials Research Society Proceedings,* Volume 926, 2006, http://journals.cambridge.org /action/displayAbstract?fromPage=online&aid=7996806.

16. www.google.com/patents?hl=en&lr=&vid= USPAT4677989&id=3ZorAAAAEBAJ&oi=fnd&dq= Lois+Robblee+iridium+oxide&printsec=abstract#v= onepage&q=Lois%20Robblee%20iridium%20oxide& f=false.

17. S. R. Otto, R. V. Shannon, E. P. Wilkinson, W. E. Hitselberger, D. B. McCreery, J. K. Moore, and D. E. Brackmann, "Audiologic outcomes with the penetrating electrode auditory brainstem implant," *Otology and Neurotology,* Vol. 29,

Number 8, Dec 2008, pp. 1147–1154, www.ncbi.nlm.nih
.gov/pubmed/18931643.

Chapter 7. Inducing Fear and Erasing Memories

1. Jim Keeley, "Learning Not to Be Afraid," *Howard Hughes Medical Institute News,* October 8, 2008, www.hhmi.org /news/learning-how-not-be-afraid.
2. Richard Gray, "Scientists Find Drug to Banish Bad Memories, *The Telegraph,* July 1, 2007.
3. Ibid.
4. Interview transcript, "Joseph LeDoux on Replacing Fear Memories," National Institute of Mental Health, January 4, 2010, www.nimh.nih.gov/media/video/ledoux.shtml.

ACKNOWLEDGMENTS

As I close this book, I'd like to express deep and sincere thanks to Marc Resnick, executive editor at St. Martin's Press. I've been fortunate to write books for Marc since 1999, and I couldn't ask for a more intelligent and insightful editor. In addition, he's a great guy with a fabulous personality, and it's always a pleasure to work for him. Thank you, Marc, for everything you've done for me and, by extension, for my children.

Thanks also to Lori Perkins, who accepted me as a client in 1996 and first introduced me to Marc and to St. Martin's Press in 1999.

I also want to thank the amazing staff at St. Martin's Press, everyone from copy editors to artists to proofreaders to publicity people to marketing folks. I'm relying on memory here, so apologies to anyone I accidentally neglect to mention. Special thanks to Sarah Lumnah, who worked with me on many of my early books, and also to Surie Rudoff and Heather Florence, two behind-the-scenes editors who make every book so much better. Special thanks to publicists Kimberly Hanson, Krysten Powell, and Katie Bassel, and to Katherine Canfield, Julie Gutin, Stephanie Davis, Joseph Goldschein, Bridget McGovern, Irene Gallo, and the entire production and marketing team. I couldn't write these books without the support of all of you.